Pwlldu Remembered

THE STORY OF
GOWER'S SMALLEST VILLAGE

Heather Holt

Published by the Author

First Impression September 1996
Second Impression October 1996
Third Impression November 1996
Fourth Impression January 1997
Fifth Impression May 1997

Second Edition October 1998

Published by the Author
390 Mumbles Road
Norton, Swansea, SA3 5TN
Telephone: (01792) 521457

ISBN 0 9529165 0 9

*Printed in Wales by
Dinefwr Press
Rawlings Road, Llandybïe
Carmarthenshire, SA18 3YD*

Cover photograph: Helen Holt

Contents

The author, Heather Holt, with Sir Glanmor Williams at the launch of the book.

Preface to the Second Edition

The response to the first edition of *Pwlldu Remembered* has been overwhelming. Not only have there been five reprints but I have received letters of appreciation from many different addresses in this country and some from Canada, America, Australia and New Zealand. From all it was obvious that this lovely bay held very special memories for them. Indeed one young couple from Wellington, New Zealand have even named their cottage Pwlldu – apparently Makara Beach shares many of the features of the Gower bay. To all my readers I should like to express the thrill and excitement as well as the many hours of enjoyment that their response has given me.

As readers will know much of the early history of Pwlldu was supplied to me by surviving members of the Jenkins family of the old 'Ship Inn'. From childhood Alf Jenkins had told me many stories which remained in my memory and in all the research for my book I had found his oral history to be remarkably accurate. On one occasion I distinctly remembered him writing slowly and painstakingly in some notebook. He even remarked to me that one day someone might read his story and young people like me would be glad to have it.

When Alf died his wife Marion inherited the cottage and of course all Alf's personal possessions. These on her death passed to Marion's family. The Jenkins family knew of the note book but had no knowledge of its whereabouts. It was thus very important that I should trace Marion's two nephews who might well be able to furnish me with more information and who might even know of the whereabouts of the notebook. The only name I was given was that of Frank Morgan one of Marion's brothers. I was told he had lived in Llanelli. In spite of strenuous efforts, to find 'a Morgan' in Llanelli proved impossible! I just had to carry on and publish the book using the material I had.

Then six months ago, two years after the book had been published, on a Sunday morning I answered the door and there was Mr Frank Mathews, whose mother had been Marion's sister. He had found me! Later the same week I met other members of the family including Mr George Morgan, the other 'missing' nephew. They were able to supply me with some lovely new photographs and some fascinating details of 'Ship' which they had visited so often in their childhood – but alas – no sign of Alf's notebook.

This is when Fate stepped in. One week before I had decided to publish a second edition of the book I telephoned Mr Frank Mathews to confirm a few details about the photographs he had given me. "I think you had better come and see me," he said. "You see I have found Alf's notebook!"

So I felt that any new edition must contain this unique document giving us some truly remarkable details of 'The Story of Pwlldu' which was the title Alf gave his writing.

Remember this is an old man nearing the end of his life recalling various snippits of history passed on to him by his father, grandfather and great grandfather. Some of his memories are times he remembers from his own life, as a boy and a man. Often it is difficult to follow a line of thought, the sentences are disjointed as one thought quickly follows another. There are few dates and the punctuation is almost non existent. But for a man who had little or no formal education it is a remarkable piece of work; at times the prose is almost poetic, there are charming touches of humour, and the whole displays a love and enthusiasm for his subject. I felt it would be wrong to try to split it up and make corrections. Let it stand as it is – the testimony of an old man looking back on a rich and rewarding life. I hope you enjoy it as much as I did.

Together with a few extra details and photographs I felt I had to include the story of the German 'U' boat. My brother after reading the account said, "I am having nightmares as I think of those scary events going on whilst we were tucked up in bed – can you imagine what would have happened if the sub or its shore crew had been seen. Blood and bullets instead of the story of a retired old submariner somewhere in Germany taking on water for his thirsty crew!"

For

Tim, Jenni, Robert, Rebecca and Zoë

Pwlldu – an eternal place!
The black stream under the stones
Carries the bones of the dead,
The starved, the talkative bones.

Vernon Watkins

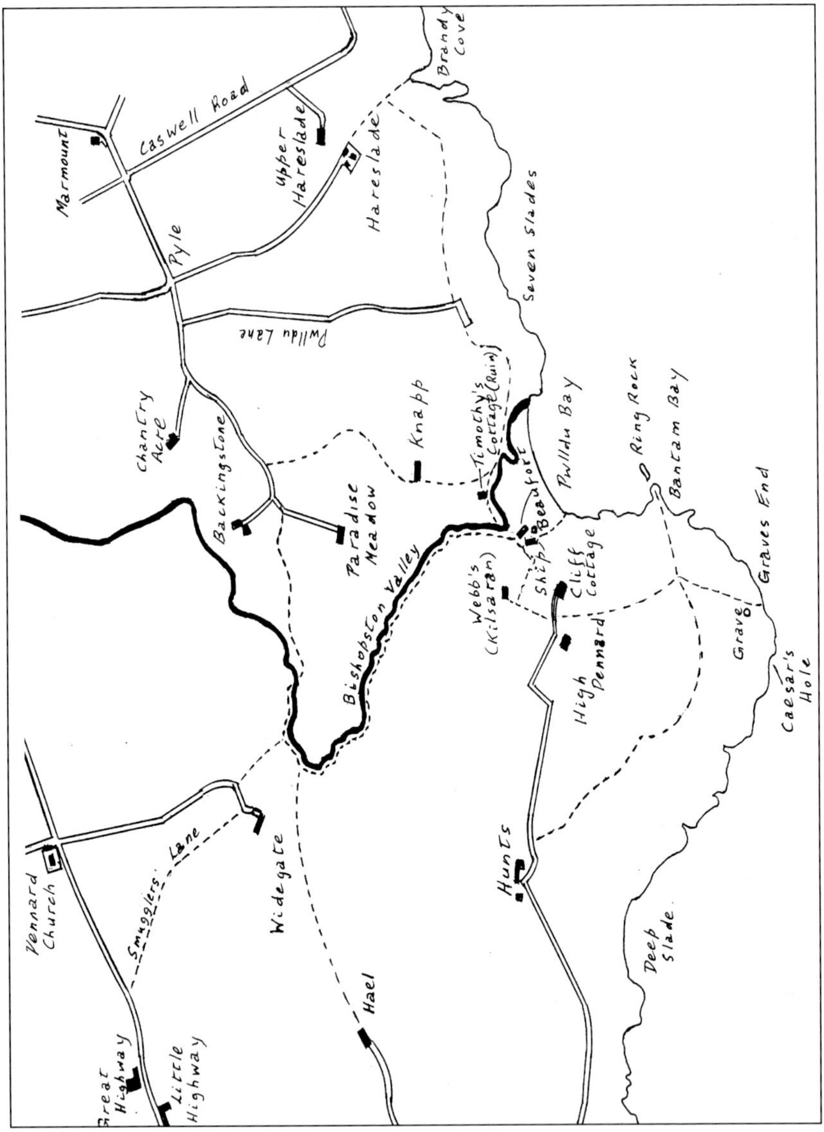
Brandy Cove
Caswell Road
Marmount
Upper Hareslade
Hareslade
Seven Slades
Pyle
Pwlldu Lane
Chantry Acre
Knapp
Timothy's Cottage (Ruin)
Pwlldu Bay
Ring Rock
Bantam Bay
Backingstone
Paradise Meadow
Beaufort
Ship
Cliff Cottage
Webb's (Kilsaran)
Graves End
Bishopston Valley
High Pennard
Grave
Caesar's Hole
Pennard Church
Smugglers' Lane
Widegate
Hunts
Deep Slade
Hael
Great Highway
Little Highway

Pwlldu and its Environs.

Introduction

This is a book I felt I had to write. My grandfather, the well-known Swansea garage proprietor, Mr. Ivor L. Roberts, had leased from Mrs Gilbertson one of the oldest cottages in High Pennard. Cliff Cottage stands on its own, tucked into the high cliff directly overlooking the Bay. Since the late 1930's it had been part of our family life.

My whole life has been bound up in some way with the people and landscape of Pwlldu. I had learnt to swim in the calm, deep waters of Needles Bay. All my week-ends and holidays were spent living in the cottage. During the last years of the second World War I lived there full time. I walked to Parkmill School across the cliffs in all kinds of weather. My childhood days were idyllic; making dens in the old quarry; helping on the farms; crabbing on the rocks, and swimming in the bay.

In college days, numerous student friends joined me in hilarious 'country' week-ends. Not even put off by the 'earth-closet' which was daily emptied and duly dug into the garden; we walked the cliffs; read poetry and drama, spread-eagled on the flat Needles rocks; swam, crabbed, returning exhausted to curl up in front of the huge open fire, lit from logs which had been painfully carried up from the beach.

This is the place where my husband and I got to know and love each other; my engagement ring being finally placed on my finger in the splendid isolation of Bantam Bay, the other side of the great Needles rocks.

In the 1950's my two babies were born. Now after an exhausting day on the beach, we would climb the steep path and the long slope leading to the cottage. A tired toddler would be perilously perched on my husband's shoulders, while we carried between us a carry cot which became increasingly heavy as my hefty son grew. I fed my two babies in the front upstairs sitting room of Beaufort House, lovingly watched over by the two James sisters: Aunty 'Ru' and 'Aunty Maud'.

In Ship lived Alf and 'Ma' Jenkins, both of whom had been an intimate part of my childhood and now were equally interested in my own children.

Then in 1959 the dreadful blow came. Mrs Gilbertson had died some years earlier and the lease for 'Cliff Cottage' was up. We thought that we would be able to renew the lease without any trouble. But Mrs Vivian who had inherited the cottage together with many other of the surrounding farms and cottages, informed us that the property was required for one of her estate workers. This was the only way we could be forced to leave the cottage after such a long tenancy. In vain my husband went to see Mrs Vivian and plead our case. I can still remember the desolate feeling of utter despair when I was given the news that we had to leave Cliff Cottage. Was this to be the end of my precious connection with Pwlldu?

For several years we tried visiting other parts of Gower, even locating a caravan on Horton Bay.

Then out of the blue, we heard from close friends, that the Beaufort Inn was for sale. On our own we knew we could not afford to buy it, already having taken out a sizeable mortgage on our Swansea home. But with two other families, it might just be possible.

So on a wonderfully sunny morning, in July 1971, three families gathered on the top lawn of Beaufort and made a momentous decision. While the others pondered on difficulties of finance, the problems of sharing; I just knew I had to have it. Later in the privacy of our own home, while my husband made urgent appointments to see bank managers and arrange mortgage facilities, I remained calm and completely confident that we would, and indeed we *had* to buy a share in Beaufort. After all, I was coming 'home'. Pwlldu had been for so long a part of my very existence. To return to my links was a necessity.

So, with my roots once more firmly planted in this magical place, I began to remember the many stories of the valley, the stirring tales of yesteryear that had been given in response to my questions over the years.

Then my grand-children started asking questions, and as I attempted to answer them, I began to realise that perhaps the time had come to try and write as much as I could of the strange and unique history of this 'eternal place'.

This proved to be a more difficult task than I had first realised. The history of the families in the big manor-houses such as Penrice and Kilvrough had been successfully written many times. These people wrote and kept letters and even diaries, preserved the estate account-book, and when they died were buried in vaults or inside the church under handsome and informative monuments. Their houses, altered or enlarged by successive owners, reflect changing customs and interests, and often follow the changes of architectural fashion. But in the Valley of Pwlldu and the cliffs of Pennard and Bishopston, the inns, farmhouses and surviving cottages were built according to almost ageless tradition. Reminders of what must have gone can still be seen in a renovated cottage or a scarred landscape, but very seldom was any record kept.

I have had to rely on careful memory, uncluttered by any printed news. "My grand-dad used to tell how his grand-dad . . ." might be said to the speaker's grandchild and span seven generations – 200 years or more.

To some extent my task was made easier because of the unique position of this isolated valley which for centuries had been cut off from the rest of Gower. Swansea had always been only six miles away as the crow flies, but before roads were made, it might well have been another country. Indeed in the eighteenth and early nineteenth century it was the sea that was the main highway, and the coasts of Devon immediately opposite Pwlldu were more accessible than the rest of Wales.

In the majority of homesteads the same families had lived, loved, married and squabbled for over a hundred years. It is largely from the lips of these people that I have gathered together the threads of my story. Doubtless there are those that will dispute the accuracy of some parts of this history. Throughout the ages the tales will have been added to or at least exaggerated. But I felt that it was important to rescue their stories from what, in a very short time, will be oblivion.

Wherever possible I have tried to check these accounts with the few written records that do exist, and on the whole, I have found the 'oral memories' to be remarkably accurate.

The people in my story revealed themselves as instinctively individual characters, self reliant, intelligent, gritty men and women with a wicked sense of humour. Their life before 1900 was often frugal, fraught with all kinds of disaster, ill health and infant mortality. Yet this isolated community drew strength from each other. With little or no education, and none of the basic luxuries that we now take for granted, they still managed to live full, rich lives, with dignity and realism. As their stories unfolded I realised more and more that here was a community of ordinary men and women, who often fought hard battles with poverty and adversity, but rarely allowed themselves to be beaten or daunted.

Of course after 1900, with the cessation of quarrying and smuggling, farming became more important. The spectacular scenery of this hidden valley in Gower began to attract walkers and artists. The two inns in the valley, in different ways tried to meet the demands of this new clientele.

The life of the farmers, their workers and families who still lived in the same cottages as their ancestors, changed but little. Their lives were lived in the main as they had been for some 500 years. Because of the isolation of the valley, the lack of roads and easy transport, changes were even longer coming to Pwlldu than much of the rest of Gower. Indeed I would say that even as late as the 1950's life in Pwlldu and High Pennard went on in much the same way; and this has enabled me to 'rescue' with the aid of tape recording much of its fascinating history from people now in their eighties or nineties who have been able to give me reliable accounts of life in their early childhood.

So this book has been a long time in the writing. I have been collecting facts, anecdotes, photographs and 'taped' interviews for many years. Now for my five grand-children, I feel the time has come to try to set this fascinating story down to paper. I hope you enjoy it!

Early Years

The boundary of the Parishes of Bishopston and Pennard is the bed of the Bishopston stream which flows down the valley into Pwlldu Bay. So to unravel any history of Pwlldu, it is necessary to look at the records of both parishes; and to call upon memories of families living in the Pwlldu Valley itself; or in the farms and cottages, located on top of the towering cliffs on either side of the Bay.

Pennard parish formed part of the Lordship of Gower. The boundaries go back to the twelfth century when the Normans began to make their presence felt in Gower. The first Lordship of Gower was conferred on Henry de Newburgh, Earl of Warwick, by Henry I in 1106. In order to consolidate his hold over his possessions, he built castles at strategic points and created manors within the Lordship, which he then bestowed on his followers. Thus a Manor of Pennard was created and an early wooden castle was built near or upon the site of the present ruin.

The Lords of Gower hoped to maximise the value of their holdings with as little trouble and expense as possible. They were used to a well developed feudal system under which tenants and retainers held lands in exchange for services, and the farming was done on a communal basis centred upon a village. In Pennard, the feudal system was introduced based on services and this part of Gower was known as 'English Gower' where feudalism and Anglo Norman law were introduced.

As the years passed, the feudal system broke down. Pennard had never been a valuable Manor compared with many of those in England. There were frequent political upheavals and after the 'besanding' its value was further decreased. The Lords of the Manor of Pennard began to allow their overseers to manage their estates; they were content just to receive their various feudal dues and rents.

In 1321, the De Breos family finally disposed of its Manor and William de Breos granted to his huntsman, his wife and heirs the full liberty to hunt in the sandy wastes of his Manor. The same huntsman received land from William, remembered in Hunt's Farm which is situated half way along the cliff, between Pwlldu Head and Pennard.

It is shortly after this time that new areas began to open up to the east of the parish, and new farms such as Hunts, Hael, and Widegate. One of these new areas was doubtless High Pennard, where quarrying was by the 17th century a lively coastal trade. As early as 1650 in the Oliver Cromwell Survey, there is mention of limestone quarrying in a place called 'Cutters Wout'. This could be the Pwlldu quarry which was situated directly under Pwlldu Head, and ran right down to the beach itself.

It is difficult to assess accurately the population of Pennard at this time, but Mr. H. R. J. Davies has done some excellent work in this area, and come up with some interesting figures. The first Subsidy Assessment Roll for the Swansea Hundred of 1543 lists 42 persons for assessment in the Pennard parish. Assuming an average of 4.3 persons per household, this gives us a rough estimate of 180 people living in the parish. Making similar deductions from the Cromwellian Survey of 1650, it seems that the population had risen to about 215 people. The main settlements of the parish at the time were Kittle (13 houses), Southgate (10), High Pennard (9) and Highway (3); so High Pennard at this time was almost as big as the other areas, and this was without doubt because of the quarrying at Pwlldu.

Isaac Hamon in 1697 reported basic changes taking place in the economic and social life of the region. Farming was becoming more prosperous, and the families in Pwlldu, High Pennard, Kittle, and the neighbouring farms of Bishopston, were eking out their livelihood with the quarrying of limestone and the odd bit of smuggling. Let us begin by looking at the latter.

Smuggling

One of the nine houses in the area of High Pennard during the 17th century was undoubtedly the Ship Inn. From the old Pennard Parish records we know that the Jenkin family was already resident in the inn by 1730 and very possibly much earlier. Alf Jenkins was a direct descendant of John Jenkin who lived in Pwlldu at this time. As a child I had listened many times to the stirring tales of his ancestors which had been passed down to him by his father and grandfather. His 'memories' have helped to bring to life this exciting era in the history of Pwlldu.

John Jenkin would have been just one of the many men who became smugglers; they would have all been drawn from the small closely knit community of 'Pwlldye', High Pennard, and Bishopston Valley. These farmers, fishermen, innkeepers, and quarrymen were known as 'country people' by the Customs Officials. By the locals they were simply known as 'The Men'.

Alf Jenkins had assured me that *"it was the best place on the whole of Gower"*. When the tide was full in, the shelving beach protected by the tall, spiky rocks of the Needles, made a natural harbour. The boats could come right up the beach, and the contraband, always referred to as 'the goodies', was quickly landed and spirited away on the backs of pack horses up the Bishopston Valley. Furthermore the absence of roads, together with the geographical position of the almost hidden valley with its steep protecting cliffs, meant that this small community was well away from prying eyes. Indeed it was the sea that was their main thoroughfare, and it was from the sea that they were to receive such a rich supplement to their meagre incomes.

These people considered smuggling as an old established

custom; it mattered little to them that it was in defiance of the law. Anyway the law itself belonged to a far-away, foreign government, that was no business of theirs. In 1817, Edward Davies, the rector of Bishopston, published a sermon entitled 'Public dues Obligatory on a Christian Conscience'. In it he pointed out the sinfulness of smuggling which was an act of disloyalty to the king; while the illicit trade in spirits led to the evils of drink. Unfortunately his words had little or no impact on his parishioners. Why should they have to pay heavy duties on the few luxuries that made their drab lives more bearable – brandy, rum and tobacco.

By 1776 armed vessels belonging to smuggling syndicates brought in brandy and wine from France, and tobacco, tea, salt and soap from Ireland. Many of these rich cargoes were brought into Pwlldu Bay in broad daylight with little chance of interference.

The Gower Coast as a whole was proving to be a constant nightmare for the Swansea Officers. From contemporary records it would seem that the Revenue Men were too busy squabbling among themselves to worry about smuggling.

We know that in 1759 at Porthcawl a vessel had discharged vast quantities of sugar, coffee and cocoa – but no rum and brandy! A local officer on questioning the country people about why no spirits had been landed, was calmly told that these had already been unloaded on a small bay near Swansea – *"there was a better market for spirits at that place"*. This could well have been the appropriately named Brandy Cove, which in the previous century had been known as Hareslade Cove; but it was more likely to have been Pwlldu Bay, where many of the larger smuggling operations were taking place.

The man most likely to be in charge of the operation was William Hawkin Arthur, the 'Mr Big' of this highly lucrative trade. He had a great reputation as a smuggler. The Parish Registers, which date from 1750, tell us that only a few years previously a tree had been cut down on which a Customs officer had been shot while watching his prey. In 1784 the burial is recorded of *"William Hawkin Arthur of Highway, in this Parish"*. His son, William Arthur (Jun.) who was no less a successful 'free trader', stepped into his shoes. The family was originally from Devon. They had established themselves in Pennard, at Highway, the present Highway Farm .The Swansea Guide for 1802 tells us of *"the Highway Mansion House belonging to William Arthur Esq., a proprietor of considerable stone-coal and culm quarries on the Swansea Canal"*. It could well be that his clandestine work funded his quarries. On the face of it, he was a highly respectable business man who probably attended Pennard Parish church on a regular basis. It is in that church's records of 1784 that we are reminded that even highly successful men still had to endure the not uncommon tragedy of infant mortality:

> *1784 – William Hawkin, Son of William and Grace Arthur, born May 17th, baptised June 6th, buried Novenber 13th.*

The very nature of his clandestine work meant that only on rare occasions when the smugglers were caught red-handed were their activities reported in the newspapers or became part of the official Customs Reports.

Arthur was running the most successful gang of smugglers to operate in Gower. He lived in Great Highway, while his Deputy, John Griffiths, lived at Little Highway, another farm situated on the opposite side of the Pennard Road and a very short distance from Arthur's home. In the nave of Pennard Church there are three tablets, one of which is in memory of a John Griffiths of Highway, who died in 1780, age 54. This family is mentioned in parish documents as early as the 15th century. In the same way that William Arthur had taken over from his father, John Griffiths's son continued in his father's role, as William Arthur's right hand man. These two Gower farmhouses, Highway and Little Highway, became the centre of the smuggling operations; their outbuildings were used as storehouses for smuggled goods and distributing centres for the whole countryside. The 'stuff' was landed at Brandy Cove and Pwlldu and hauled by pack-horses up Bishopston Valley, then along the significantly named Smugglers Lane to Highway.

For many years the lane was overgrown and virtually impassable, but it has now been cleared and can be safely negotiated on foot. As you proceed between the tall banks you are virtually hidden from the surrounding fields and it is easy to imagine the many files of horses and men that would have passed along its length with their illicit cargoes. It is little wonder that the three isolated Revenue Officers, who for many years were the only men employed to guard the extended coasts of Gower, could do little to prevent this highly lucrative trade.

The Arthur and the Griffiths families had enjoyed possibly forty years of profitable trading before any serious attempt was made to curb .their activities. The local inhabitants, of course, were involved to a man, and it is safe to say that the procession of pack-horses that padded their way along Smugglers' Lane included every horse from the surrounding farms. The only folk not in the know were the Excise Men. There is little doubt that drinkers at the Ship bar were regularly served with illicit spirits that had been landed at the bay, while 'Highway' became the best-known location for smuggled goods in the whole of Gower.

If it so happened that West Gower folk ran out of liquid refreshment before the next cargo was due at Porteynon or Rhossilli, cellars were replenished from Highway. On one occasion, Farmer 'T' of Horton was returning home at dead of night through Penrice lanes when he was accosted by Preventative Men. Mindful of the keg of brandy strapped by the cantle of his saddle, he promptly forsook the stirrups for the safety of the nearest hedge, taking to his heels across country. His horse, of course, was forfeit, but its ownership was never established.

A traditional story is told of Arthur's resourcefulness. A lieutenant and two riding officers once called at Highway with a search warrant. Arthur and his henchmen, of course, protested, but the customs men found an odd keg of best geneva hidden in a loft. The lieutenant, considering this evidence enough to apprehend William Arthur, despatched his men to requisition a horse. Fearing that the keg might in some way

or other disappear from under his nose, he promptly sat upon it and awaited the return of his subordinates. In the meantime Arthur instructed his servants to create and sustain a terrific din under the loft while he drilled an augerhole through the floor and into the keg, thereby draining the liquor. The lieutenant sat tight, believing that the noises were created to entice him away from his capture.

When the riding officers returned and proceeded to handle the keg, much to their dismay, they found it empty. No recourse was left to them other than to retreat ignominiously.

Another occasion when Arthur snapped his fingers at authority was in 1786, when the Customs at Swansea got wind that a 'run' was to be made that afternoon at Pwlldu. That evening an optimistic band of fourteen Revenue officers surrounded Great Highway on the Pennard Road, and called on William Arthur to surrender. Finding the premises silent and apparently deserted, they knocked at the door. A sleepy voice refused them admittance, denying all knowledge of contraband, but doubtless keen eyes were assessing their strength. Suddenly a gang of masked men, some fifty in number, rushed out. They were armed with pokers, iron bars, large knives, building bricks and other offensive weapons. The unarmed Revenue Men were quickly overpowered and rolled in the filth of the farmyard. It had been quite impossible to serve any kind of writ on Arthur. A disconsolate and evil-smelling company plodded silently back to Swansea.

Customs sought the help of the army but were only told *"the situation at present would not admit any attachment being sent to S. Wales."*

That the smuggling continued unabated for the next few years is confirmed by a brief report that appeared in *The Cambrian* dated 1789, where it is recorded that Arthur was fined £5.5.0 for "harbouring and concealing prohibited goods."

The Island of Lundy had long been the centre of smuggling operations. Many coastal traders would call at the Island to pick up contraband which had come from France and Ireland. Under the leadership of a dastardly character named Doggett, the island was a 'no-go' area for Customs Officers who knew the fierce and deadly opposition they would face if they attempted any kind of landing. When Doggitt reached the age of fifty-five he retired from the island. However, the Customs had little time to feel relieved, because within six months Arthur had transferred some of his operations onto the vacant island.

One of the vessels owned by William Arthur was 'The Cornwall'. This ship regularly went out to meet incoming vessels in the Channel. On many occasions it had been rummaged by the Customs but nothing was found. However in 1782, on yet another search, four and a half ankers of brandy and six bags of tea were found hidden under the forecastle. The vessel was seized and ultimately condemned, suffering the usual fate of being sawn into three pieces.

Trade continued to prosper exceedingly for another nineteen years and Arthur was able to buy an estate near Hartland in Devonshire, where possibly he established another smuggling centre. In his absence John Griffiths organised the landings at Pwlldu and the disposal of goods.

When the spring of 1804 arrived, nothing had happened to arouse any hope in the hearts of the Preventative Men that they would ever get on even terms with Arthur, and to Arthur and his assistants there was no indication that their long-established trade would ever be disturbed. And then, in one night as a result of a dramatic incident the whole smuggling business at Great and Little Highway Farms became a thing of the past.

It must be explained that other and greater events had occurred during the intervening years. The French Revolution had embroiled nations; the sinister figure of Napoleon Bonaparte was preparing at Boulogne for the invasion of England; and around our coasts volunteer corps were formed to resist such an invasion. The corps formed in Gower was part of the Glamorgan Sea Fencibles under the command of Lieutenant Samuel Sawyer, R.N.

One April afternoon in 1804, Lieutenant Sawyer and Customs Officer Beavan were on patrol on the beach at Oxwich. Their boats were especially licensed and they were allowed to carry arms. On this particular evening Sawyer and Beavan sighted a cutter coming into the bay and come to anchor. In a short time two men could be seen approaching the shore in a small boat. On landing on the beach the two men approached the Officers and asked for the whereabouts of 'Highway' – it seems quite unbelievable that this should happen. Much to their credit Sawyer and Beavan kept their wits and calmly told them it was just around the headland to Pwlldu head.

The officers were now aware that a landing was to be effected that night. To keep their own counsel was imperative, for Gower was a whispering gallery. It was not until 10 p.m. that they took into their confidence Francis Beavan, son of the Customs Officer and a member of the Sea Fencibles. To him they suggested the commission of riding round by Parkmill and returning past the two suspected farms. This involved danger, for if the smugglers were at work and he was recognised when passing Great Highway, he might be trapped before he could get beyond Little Highway.

It was not until 2 a.m. that Francis Beavan returned. He reported that smugglers were depositing casks of spirits at both farms; that groups of horsemen with lanterns were before each, and that in the darkness and confusion he had slipped through without being recognised. Immediately Sawyer called out members of the Sea Fencibles and, with Beavan, took to the road. It was arranged that as they would come to Little Highway first, Sawyer and a party should halt there whilst Beavan and his party pushed on to Great Highway.

At Little Highway Sawyer found the landing still in progress. Casks littered the farmyard, forms of horses loomed in the shadows cast from lanterns, whilst a stream of light came from the open doorway. But when Sawyer reached that door it was slammed in his face, and no answer was given to his demand for admittance.

He knew that somewhere in that house were places of concealment and all traces of contraband were being removed. At length the door was opened and Sawyer and his men commenced their search. Although they probed from kitchen to attic they found nothing.

Nonplussed, they assembled in the kitchen, which in common with most Gower cottages had an earthenware floor. A Sea Fencible named Jones noticed an inequality in the earthen floor near the cheese-press. The probe went home, the earth was pushed aside, and the trap-door to the hidden cellar was revealed. The search was then extended to the out-houses again and a cellar full of contraband was discovered.

In the meantime, Beavan, at the neighbouring farm, was also frustrated in his quest until word reached him of Sawyer's successes. A closer scrutiny revealed similar places of concealment, first in the pig-sty and then in a concealed cellar under the barn from which Arthur had driven away the Preventative Men nineteen years before.

When the morning light came. it fell upon a large pile of casks in the farmyard of Little Highway under the guard of the Sea Fencibles.

The night's haul came to 420 casks of spirits amounting to nearly 3,000 gallons. However not all the casks arrived at the Swansea Custom House; Beavan had to leave some casks with 200 country people who were threatening the officers. As Beavan explained *"some of them were much intoxicated, very clamorous and threatening they be allowed to drink."*

This was one of the biggest seizures in Gower and really marked the beginning of the end of smuggling on a large scale. It led to the break up of Arthur and his gang. It was believed that Arthur retired to his estate in Devon. The extant registers of Pennard Parish Church of St. Mary's, date back to 1750; the entry on William Arthur is particularly interesting:

> *"William Hawkin Arthur – This family, who lived at Highway, Pennard during the latter years of the 18th century, were noted for their smuggling and other related activities. One son, whose baptism was registered here in 1774, became*

> *a country parson in Devonshire and was the father of the Naval Officer who, in 1860, surveyed the area of Liaotung Peninsular in Northern China and Port Arthur on that peninsular was named after him."*

John Griffiths died in 1780. There is a monument in the nave of St. Mary's Church, Pennard – *"To John Griffiths of Highway (a family whose recorded connection with the parish commences early in the 15th century)."*

The Griffiths family lived on in Highway for many centuries. Indeed Mr Walter Griffiths , a direct descendent now lives in Bishopston and was able to confirm many of the details of the thrilling tales of his ancestors. His father, Mr Samuel Griffiths, a councillor of long standing and a former church warden, was interviewed by the press. He was rightly quite complacent about the clandestine adventures of his forbears. As he remarked, *"any of our forbears who had lived in Pwlldu or High Pennard at that time would have been similarly implicated".* Councillor Griffiths added that *"his Hanoverian Majesty lacked for nothing, whereas Pennard folk in those days lost a lot of sleep in order to add a little excitement and comfort to an existence all too drab and dreary."*

Arthur and his gang were finished, and the following year another success for the Customs Officers was scored. George Beynon, stationed at Rhossilli Bay, surprised a gang landing goods, and although the smugglers managed to make good their escape, they were forced to leave behind over 100 casks of brandy, Gineva, and wine. The same year another huge consignment of tobacco and wine was seized. Then in 1807, a large seizure was made at Middleton, near Rhossilli. Some 30 kegs of brandy and over £1,200 worth of tobacco was found in a haystack. The tables had at last been turned on the smugglers; no operator could afford to lose such huge consignments, and it was rapidly becoming clear that the chances of successfully landing goods were becoming very thin. The Sea Fencibles of Gower were of a far higher calibre than their counterparts elsewhere.

In 1809/10 the Preventative Water Guard was established

and this was another factor in the decline of smuggling in the Bristol Channel. The new Water Guards' duty was to operate in coastal waters and attack smugglers who managed to evade Customs and Excise vessels operating further out. If the water was too rough to take out a small rowing boat, they patrolled the coast on foot and acted as a link with the riding officers.

Less than twelve months after the Preventative Guards had started to operate, the message came from Swansea *"there is no smuggling of any magnitude"* being carried out on the coasts of Gower.

But this was not the end of smuggling at Pwlldu. The 'Men' who had so enjoyed the excitement, danger and camaraderie of the smuggling gang were not likely to give it up so easily. Some smuggling did undoubtedly take place, but on a far smaller scale; and the 'goodies' were mostly distributed among the local people.

This was also the time when 'the Men' had to be careful. No more landing contraband on the beach in broad daylight. Operations had to be carried out at night, usually at midnight when there was a full moon and a full tide. There had to be a 'lookout' on the top of the cliff, ready to spot the stab of furtive blue light from the smuggling craft in the bay. It is told that a special signalling system was used by the five cottages: Ship, Beaufort Inn (which had just been built), The Webbs, Knapp Farm and Cliff Cottage. Oil lamps would be lit and placed in the windows indicating to the smugglers that the coast was clear.

C. D. Morgan writing in 1860 describes how French luggers would come into 'Pwldy' bay, discharge their cargoes at High Tide and then be quickly away.

One of the many amusing stories that have been passed down by word of mouth and which is also related by C. D. Morgan, concerns Mr Webb, probably the same Webb who lived in Webbs' Cottage (now known as 'Kilsaran') in the 1840's. He was a well-known member of the smugglers gang. After one particularly successful landing, he set off up the cliff with two ankers of brandy slung across his saddle. He had promised a tenant of one of the farms in High Pennard to bring him some cognac when he was taking some to Swansea. Arriving at the cottage, Webb offered 'Uncle John' to take a drink through a quill directly placed in the barrel that was strapped in front of the saddle. Before long his wife Nanny, and even the maid Betty, were given a long pull. The three hapless peasants just managed to get back into the cottage before collapsing in a heap on the floor. Three days and nights were to pass before passers-by were alerted by the sound of hungry and thirsty cattle. Needless to say John and Nanny never asked Mr Webb for Geneva again!

By the 1850s smuggling had been virtually wiped out. The likelihood of being caught had greatly increased, At the same time the rewards were decreasing, for the Government had adopted a free-trade policy and was steadily reducing the duties on many imported goods. Smuggling died out because it was no longer worth taking such grave risks. Yet although only the memories survived, the romance lived on. Alf Jenkins during his lifetime fascinated many regulars and visitors to the Beaufort bar with his tales of successful smuggling runs. 'Ma' Jenkins right up to the time of her death was convinced she could hear the footsteps of the horses and men coming over the pebbles after landing their cargo on a moonlit night on a full tide.

As a child, and later as a married woman with my own children, I would be greeted on a morning by Mrs Jenkins with the words, *"Did you hear 'the Men' last night?"* For years I put it all down to an old woman's superstitions and vivid imagination – that is until a certain night in the 1970's!

All the conditions for 'a landing' were there – a full moon bathed the bay with silver light. The calm sea was full in; the only sound was a gentle lapping of the waves breaking on the sand. It was a perfect night for a walk on the beach. Accompanied by my black Labrador dog, I left the garden of Beaufort and made my way over the pebbles. Suddenly, as we reached the sand, I was aware of a deadly chill in the air; my bare arms were covered with goose pimples. A low growling reached my ears, and looking down I saw Butch's fur literally standing on end, and his black lips drawn back in a fearful snarl. It is difficult to describe what I felt – not fear exactly, but certainly as if I was trapped in a time warp; and above all the conviction that I was no longer alone on the beach. Then I heard it – the unmistakable grind of pebbles moved by many feet. The whole experience lasted only seconds. The air was warm once more and Butch was barking for a stick to be thrown. Everything was back to normal.

Imagination? – too much wine at dinner? – Who knows! It was just one of the many unique Pwlldu experiences that people down the centuries have described – never frightening, but just a reminder of a past that in a very special way is still very much part of the present.

The Devon Connection

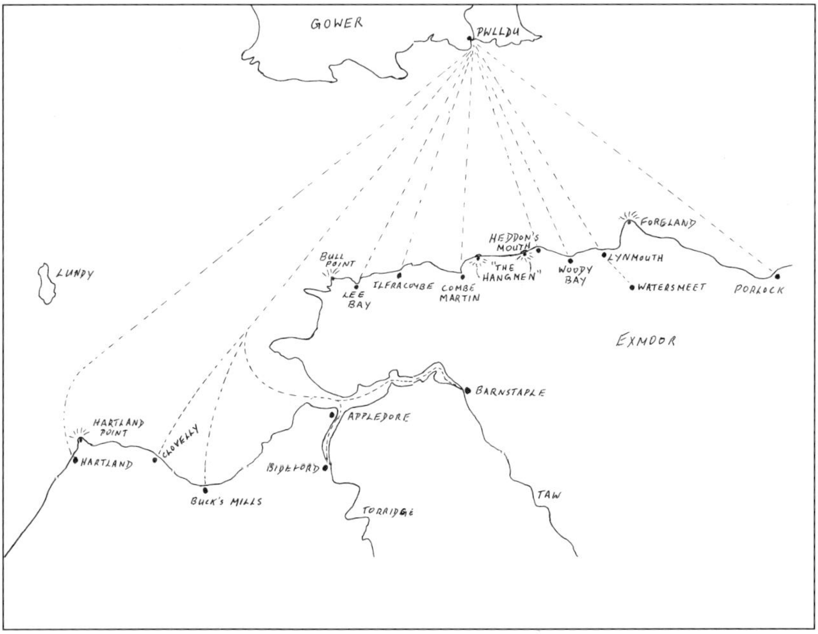

Possible destinations of Pwlldu limestone, distances from 25-45 miles by sea.

Many times I have sat on the headland at Pwlldu, gazing out to sea. On fine evenings the coastline of North Devon is clearly visible. The green heights of Exmoor; to the east Porlock Bay, and to the far west, Hartland Point (where Arthur spent his last days), can be picked out. Below, although not visible, are the twin towns of Lynton and Lynmouth. At night the cluster of pin-point lights mark out Ilfracombe. Directly opposite is the regularly flashing Foreland light. In a special way all these places are part of Pwlldu and certainly featured largely in its history. I had known this since I was a child when my grandparents had told me about the quarry and how the stones had been carried across the Channel in small sailing ships.

My parents had tried to warn us against playing in the quarry, but to no avail. Our close ally, dear 'Ma' Jenkins had provided us with candle stubs, old wooden boxes, a potentially lethal bottle of lemonade made from crystals and water from the river, and a very special treat – chocolate. This chocolate was covered in a thin film of white powder – how long it had been in stock I shudder to think. But to wartime children, chocolate was chocolate, whatever its colour. With these precious objects we set up our den in the deepest part of the old quarry workings we could find. Here were 'caves' and passages made by the repeated blastings of the limestone. As we became 'smugglers' and 'wreckers' we gave no thought to the men and women who had toiled in the quarry a hundred years or so ago.

It was not until much later in my life, when my grandchildren had started to ask questions that I decided the time had come for me to fully explore 'the Devon Connection'.

I was spurred on to do so by a rather remarkable event. On returning home from a holiday, my husband and I found a note pushed through our front door. It was signed by our next-door neighbour and rather intriguingly stated, "As soon as you arrive home, go immediately to the antique shop in Murton. They are holding something which I feel you *must* have."

When we arrived at the shop, a smiling proprietor handed us a picture. It was an unsigned but beautifully executed water colour of Pwlldu Bay. Several graceful craft were moored by ropes to the rocks in the foreground. The owners of the shop stated that they had obtained the picture locally and it had been apparently painted by an artist who had stayed at Beaufort Inn during the late nineteenth century. We bought the picture and knew that it had to return to its 'home'.

The painting was duly given a place of honour on the wall of our sitting room, the window of which framed the whole of Pwlldu, and often the coast beyond – the identical landscape of the picture.

The boats were undoubtedly the same graceful craft which had so often filled the bay in the early and middle nineteenth century. In the picture the vessels are safely moored by ropes to iron rings placed at strategic places in the rocks of the bay. These rings can still be seen today, and the largest rock of the 'Needles' formation is still known as the 'Ring' rock, because of the iron ring which protrudes from its surface. Together with the long ridge of rounded pebbles these are the remaining clues to an industry which changed both the economic and social life of 'Pwldwy' village.

I became determined to find out as much as I could about this fascinating time. I knew that to get at the real story of the people and craft that had come over from Devon, I would need to actually visit as many places as possible that might have any connection with the limestone story. The towns of Lynton and Lynmouth which are situated immediately opposite Pwlldu must have been involved. It could be that the neighbouring towns of Porlock, Barnstaple, and Combe Martin, were once receivers of Pwlldu limestone. The ships, I knew, had in the main been built at Appledore, Bideford and Barnstaple. Details of their crew and cargo could probably be obtained from the North Devon Museum. Hopefully I might be fortunate enough to come across some archive material of the time, and it was just possible that I might be able to talk with some people who not only had a special interest in this fascinating era of history but could be direct descendants of people who had worked in the industry.

Before setting off on my 'voyage of discovery', I recalled the details of the 'Pwlldu' side of the story.

Again my information was to come from many sources: the excellently written and researched articles by W. N. Jenkins and L. A. Toft which have appeared in the Gower Journals; extracts from contemporary accounts not always specifically related to Pwlldu, and of course, once again, the precious oral history passed down by the descendants of the Jenkins family of Ship and the Jones family of Beaufort, many of whom took an active part in the quarrying industry of Pwlldu.

The Story of Lime

One of its earliest uses was for liming walls, houses and out-buildings. Lime was applied on a regular basis, and apart from improving the appearance of the buildings, provided an excellent defence against the vagaries of weather and damp. W. Davies in 1815 claimed that the origin of this traditional practice was even mentioned by Aneurin, the Bard, as early as 500 AD!

It was certainly a part of the country life in Gower. In 1774, a writer on his tour of Monmouthshire and Wales commented *"there is scarcely a cottage to be seen which is not regularly brushed over every week."*

I can personally vouch for the practice carrying on in Pwll-du right through the nineteen forties and even in the fifties. All the farms and cottages in High Pennard, as well as the two Inns in the valley received a regular coating of lime, both inside and out!

The limed walls of Cliff Cottage never failed to intrigue me. When no-one was looking I would accidentally dislodge a few layers just to see the hundreds of thin layers revealed beneath – all evidence of many years of liming. One of my earliest and most vivid memories is of my uncle and father undertaking to lime the cottage. Stepladders were propped against the walls and large zinc buckets of lime precariously balanced on the top. The lime was applied with the aid of two wide paddle brushes. At the end of this hilarious operation, not only the cottage would be successfully limed but the two men as well! Their clothes and shoes would be stiff with the substance: hat and hair would be snow white and even glasses would be covered with hundreds of white spots. They appeared to have managed to get more lime on themselves than on the cottage walls!

Another not so salubrious use of lime was for keeping the earth closets clean. This was a rotten job. Each day a new trench had to be opened and then water and lime poured in and washed out. I was told that when the Beaufort was a busy pub, there were two earth closets at the bottom of the garden

'Muffies' in Pwlldu Bay c.1850 by an unknown artist.

The Bridge at Pwlldu – C. E. Schenk, 1887.

which had to serve the needs of a busy inn. The young maid was expected to clean them out twice a day. Certainly at Cliff Cottage this task was a regular chore.

Lime had also many important medicinal properties which had been known to apothecaries in previous centuries. In 1819 Abraham Rees wrote:

> *"Experience has shown limewater to be an excellent medicine in many cases; in the gravel and stone particularly. And it has also been found very serviceable in the gout, in habitual relaxations of the bowels and in other cases of relaxation. In some kinds of scurvy likewise it is of use; and it is often applied with success externally to ulcers etc."*

As medicinal knowledge advanced, its use in this way became less popular; but in country districts in the eighteenth and nineteenth centuries limewater was still being taken for minor stomach complaints. As late as 1940, I knew of two High Pennard farmers who used to use lime for the treatment of ulcers, both in cattle and people! Pwlldu folk also swore that there was no better treatment for burns than linseed oil mixed with lime.

In Pwlldu, as in the rest of Gower, access to lime was easy, as the farms themselves would be built on limestone rock. It was usual for farms to either have their own small kiln or smaller farms might well share the use of the same kiln. The Ordnance Survey Map of 1830 shows two kilns operational at Pennard. In 1879 the Survey shows three kilns operational on Pwlldu Head; while the Glamorgan Archaeological Trust shows the kiln in the fields behind the Webbs' Cottage, the ruins of which can still be seen.

The very first indication of the use of lime in agriculture is in the sixteenth century. In 1603, in his description of Pembrokeshire, George Owen of Kemes, writes:

> *"This trade of liming has been more used within these thirty or forty years (i.e. since 1560 or 70) than in times past – and*

Ruins of limestone kiln behind Kilsaran.

> *it brings forth a fine and sweet grass – and has greatly enriched those that used it."*

Risdon, writing about 1630, comments:

> *". . . of late a new invention has sprung up and been practised, by burning lyme and incorporating it for a season with earth, and then spread upon the arable land, hath provided a plentiful increase of all sorts of grain amongst us, where formerly such never grew in man's living memory."*

This mixing of lime with soil was a very common practice in Gower and the mixture was known as marl.

In Cromwell's survey of 1650, reference was made to the *"customary tenants of Penard to use, dig or break up 'all manner of Quarries of Stone at their pleasures, without any lycense of the Lord."*

The Land Sweetener

Either side of the Channel, this burning of lime for agricultural purposes expanded during the eighteenth century. It is true that very few facts are recorded, but without doubt the limeless soils of Somerset and Devon were enriched yearly as supplies of this special manure began to make an impact on cultivation yields. Burnt lime adds calcium compounds to the soil, thus neutralising acidity which was especially prevalent on the Culm Measures of Devon. It was also known to improve the drainage on clay soil which is common on the North Devon coast. So more and more Devon farmers were dressing their fields with lime; indeed the use of lime as a manure became almost obsessional in parts of Devon.

Where was this lime to come from? Limestone in large quantities was not to be found in North Devon. Even where local limestone was found, it could only be used in that locality because of the difficulties of transport. This was the case in Combe Martin, where although there were outcrops of limestone which was used in the kilns, it still had to be supplemented with supplies from Wales.

The only roads available were nothing more than narrow twisting lanes. During the last century the only method of delivering heavy goods was by sea. The farmers of North Devon had to look across the Bristol Channel to Wales and the Gower Peninsular in particular, where they knew there was a continuous band of limestone extending to the coast. Burnt lime was known to have a corrosive effect on timber, and so it could not be carried in the wooden ships of the eighteenth and early nineteenth century. The limestone in its natural state had to be shipped from quarries on the Gower Peninsular and Caldy Island and burnt at its destination.

Thus began a major industry, which was to link the hard working agricultural community, with a special breed of seamen, who plied the treacherous Bristol Channel in their small vessels to carry the limestone to North Devon.

After 1600, this trade began to grow in order to meet the growing demands of Devon farmers. Records I found in the

North Devon Maritime Museum revealed that in 1682 no fewer than 328 voyages were made to bring limestone, coal and culm to North Devon from South Wales.

The Quarry at Pwlldu

It is likely that limestone had been exported from the quarry as early as 1700 when the first cargoes were probably carried in fishing vessels. As early as 1703 there is a record of a limestone boat with quarry implements being driven ashore and wrecked. The boat was owned by a Pembrokeshire widow.

In 1808, Vancouver in his book *Agriculture of Devon* states that Oxwich, Mumbles and 'Poolridge' are suppliers of limestone to Devon. The interesting change of the word 'Pooldy' to 'Poolridge' implies that the first signs of a storm beach made from the waste pebbles left over from the quarrying process, were already in place. By 1815 the export of limestone was in full swing. W. Davies wrote: "A great trade is carried on all along the coast of Gower in Glamorganshire" and one of the most important limestone ports was Pwlldu Bay.

I attempted to trace the passage of this limestone from Pwlldu across the sea to Devon. From both sides of the Channel a fascinating picture began to emerge, of an exceptionally hard working, knowledgeable band of people, engaged in an industry which provided seasonal work for almost the whole community in Pwlldu, High Pennard, and surrounding areas; whilst across the water in Devon, there were many towns where nearly half the population was involved in this industry in one way or another.

As with smuggling, the geographical position of Pwlldu played an important part in its success as a quarry and a limestone port. Its wide, fairly steep beach, sheltered by the Needles, provided a perfect deep natural harbour for small boats. The rocks of the bay as already noted, could be used to secure the vessels. The quarry itself was immediately above the deeply hanging cliffs, down which the limestone could be carried by its own momentum to the Lower Quarry or 'Flats', to the beach where it could be loaded directly into the waiting vessels.

In the Land Tax Returns of 1775, John Jenkin is referred to as "Landlord of Pooldie House"; he was also undoubtedly involved in Arthur's smuggling adventures; but whether he had time to carry out some quarrying is unknown. However, his sons, David, George, and Hezekiah were all quarrymen, as was Alf's father David Jenkins, Junior, (1850-1929), who saw the closure of the quarry at the turn of the century. Alf, himself, remembered seeing the last of the limestone boats in the bay. Because the same family lived on in Pwlldu for at least 250 years, their folk memory is liable to be very accurate. I was privileged to talk to Alf about the quarrying on many occasions. As a child it was almost like a romantic fairy-tale, but later as an adult, both my husband and I were able to ask relevant questions, and as a result, gained some fascinating details of this important industry.

The passages and caves we played in as children, were the remains of the blasting operations that took place, usually in the winter time, when it was too rough for the boats to come in for their cargo of limestone. Alf showed us the heavy iron sledgehammers and chisels that had been used to prise out the large pieces of stone. This was after the blasting had taken place.

Leaning against the kitchen wall of The Ship (as Pooldie House came to be known) stood a long steel pole, thicker in the middle (sometimes a canon ball was used) in order to give extra weight. The pole was chiselled at one end and pointed at the other. As a child I remember being very amused at the name given to this strange implement: a jumper! Water was used to keep the head of the bar cool, and soften the stone. I was amazed to learn that it could take two days to drill 15 to 18 inches. The hole complete, it was next filled with gun-powder. Apparently David Jenkins always carried his powder in a cow's horn, which he slung across his shoulder. They would then fuse it and blow out a couple of tons of rock After the explosion, the large stones were placed in heaps, ready to be transported down the cliff to the rocks of the beach below. The stones would usually be rolled down, sometimes with the aid of iron bars; and there have been some references made

Pwlldu Quarry and 'slides'.

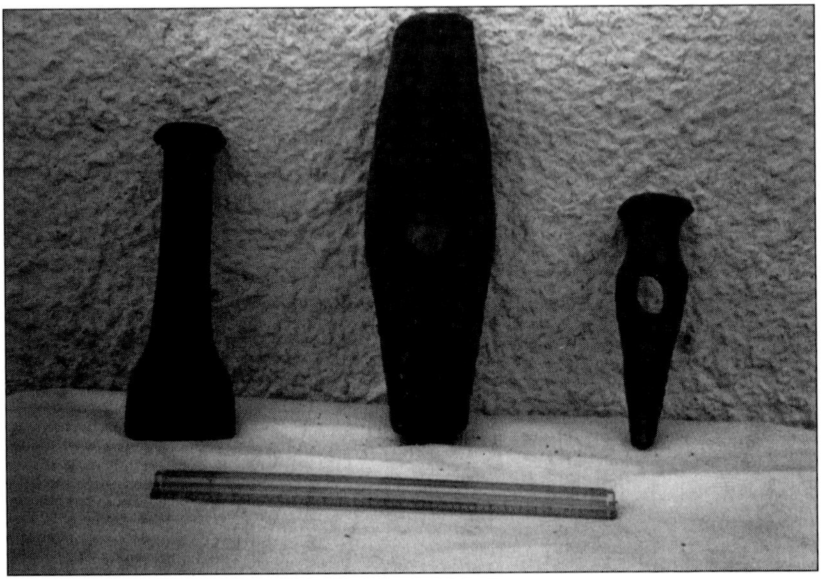

Quarrying tools.

to some kind of wheeled sledges being used, an example of which can be seen in the foreground of Schenk's painting of the Bay.

Over the centuries, the passage of these heavy stones have carved out remarkably deep trenches with high ridges on either side. These extend almost the whole width of the bay on the West side. Above the 'slides', which is what they were called, lie many groups of strangely shaped rocks like so many modern sculptures. Some of the huge boulders hang perilously between towers of rocks looking as if they could fall at any moment. Today, these unique features give the bay its almost surrealist landscape.

Each of these 'slides', sometimes known as 'quars', belonged to one man or sometimes a group of farm labourers who had formed their own working gang. Many of the workers, both men and women, would have walked over the cliffs from the cottages and farms of Pennard or even Parkmill. Others would have made their way along the floor of the valley from Kittle and Bishopston. It is even said that prisoners from Swansea Prison worked in the quarry. As the industry prospered, more than a hundred men and women were employed all the year round.

At the bottom of the cliff, the larger stones would be broken up to a more manageable size, by the use of 'sledges' (sledge hammers). The stones could be anything from 8 to 20 inches in diameter. At the end of each slide a temporary wooden staging would be built. This staging would be known as a 'flot quar'(floating quarry). Two poles were then placed either end to mark the bows and stern, ready for loading. *"This is when the women came into their own,"* said Alf Jenkins, with a glint of laughter in his eyes,*"they would lift the stones to their knees in order to pass them to the men on the staging."* It would seem that on both sides of the Channel the women were expected to do the most back-breaking jobs! (Nothing changes!!) These women, often known as 'shifters', were usually relatives of the quarrymen. They would wear canvas shirts and thick leather gloves for what was a hard and dirty job.

A practice which would appear unique to 'Pooldy Quarry'

is the loading of the stones through water. I was assured by both Alf and Hezekiah Jenkins that the boats would be sunk on the ebbing tide, by the removal of the sea cocks. When the boats were partially filled with water, by the advancing tide, the heavy stones could be lowered into the holds through the water, thus reducing any risk of damage to the structure of the boat itself. When the loading operation was completed and the water drained out at low tide, the cocks would be replaced and the vessel refloated on the next tide.

We know that loads of 60 tons or more would be taken on board a smack. This meant a heavy, long day's toil for labourers working in small groups. Short breaks were taken by the loaders, the 'lowance time' but it was strenuous work even for strong men and women.

When examining archive material in the Bideford Maritime Museum, I came across a most amusing anecdote written by one of the stone heavers of the time. C. W. Slater relates how one loader resolved publicly to become a teetotaller if he could not load up a smack entirely on his own, without the aid of alcohol refreshment. Failure meant that he would have to continue to carry on loading, without his usual consumption of strong drink. Supported by his wife, who supplied him with meals and non-intoxicating beverages during the short rest periods, he successfully completed the self-imposed Herculean operation, to the amazement and admiration of his fellow stone porters and friends. By evening, he had been involved in about 180 loading and tipping activities before he finally finished filling the vessel's hold with some 60 tons of stones.

The site of this incredible feat is not given, and it is highly unlikely that it occurred in Pwlldu Bay! But it does give us a glimpse of the very special characters of the 'stone heavers' (as they were called); indeed they could well be called 'a breed apart'; this observation will be further ratified when we look at the activities of their 'brothers' and 'sisters' across the Channel.

The lime Captains in charge of the boats would pay 1s per ton, or a set amount for a cargo; there was also a duty of 2d, and in some places 1d in each shilling, which had to be paid by the captains to the Lord of the Manor.

A very important part of these payments was the beer allowance, which was given to men and women. Alcohol was almost a necessity to the work force, for both quarry workers and sea-men. Both belonged to a hardy race of men and women who were known for feats of strength and endurance, and they had a thirst to go with their hardy life-style. C. D. Morgan in his book of 1860 tells us that "Old Will Beynon, who called his head a pimple, could drink a quart of beer in a drought, or empty the contents of a 'Long Tom' at a sitting."

At the height of the lime trade boom, there could well be as many as thirty boats in the bay, usually with a crew of two or three men; so the drinking population of Pwlldu could easily swell to some two hundred souls. One small Inn would not be able to ensure a supply of good home brewed beer for all those who needed it.

This is, without doubt, why the Beaufort was built. In the 1851 Census, Sam Jones is 'mine host' at Beaufort and is described as a victualler. Staying at Beaufort are men whose occupations are variously given as mariners and agricultural labourers. In the 1871 Census, the Jones family are described as Quarryman, Quarryman's wife and Quarryman's daughter.

So we have a picture of a very hard working, close community of quarrymen and women, together with sailors and agricultural workers, whose drink, and probably food, and even on times accommodation, would be supplied by the two Inns – Ship and later Beaufort, situated immediately opposite each other at the very edge of Pwlldu Bay.

Several of the older people who lived in the Bay have assured me that the Ship Inn was frequented by the local farmers and quarrymen , whilst Beaufort was the home of the sailors. This of course was while Ship was still an Inn. It has also been rumoured that at one time there were as many as five public houses in the Valley. H. M. Tucker and J. C. Woods in their guides to Gower, written at the turn of the century, actually name two: The Bull and the New Inn. Other local people seem to remember a third, The Star. These inns, however, were not actually in the valley. The Cross Inn was the original name of the Bishopston Valley Hotel. There was also an inn called the New Inn which was in reality, a cottage overlooking the Bishopston Valley in the village of Bishopston. A likely explanation of other remembered drinking premises is that names were given to many unlicensed alehouses, which were just cottages, brewing their own beer and readily supplying drink to those who wanted it. One such cottage was the Webbs', which was known to supply food and drink for over a century.

The Carters and Limeburners of Devon had the same grindingly hard life as the Pwlldu people, and in the same way felt they needed alcohol to help them get through a hard day's work. As Beaufort and other inns had grown up to meet the needs of the Pwlldu workers, the old Friendship Inn (now a farmhouse) was a well frequented ale house situated on the old ridgeway along Bralton Down, which became known as the 'Liming Road'. This inn had a little window through its eastern wall, at about shoulder height from the road. This was known as the Carters Bar in much the same way as the Quarryman's Bar was known in Ship Inn at Pwlldu. Unlike the Pwlldu worker, who could usually snatch enough time to sit at a bar and enjoy a pint, the carters who would be returning with laden butts from the coast, could not spare the time to actually enter the bar. They paid their pence and could then drain their tankards, without letting go of the horses' reins.

The Arrival of the 'Muffies'

As soon as the Spring weather arrived, usually sometime in early March, the first sails would be seen on the horizon. Runners would go around the cliff tops on either side of the bay: High Pennard, Knapp, Hareslade etc. hiring heavers who would help load up the boats. These heavers were paid 2 shillings a tide in Rhossilli and it was very probably a similar sum that was given to the workers at Pwlldu. This does not seem much for such back breaking work, but when one realises that a man would only earn as much as this for a full day's work on a farm, then it is obvious why they were never short of volunteers. Word would swiftly spread that the 'muffies' were on their way. This was the affectionate name given by the North Devon sailors to the rather special craft which had evolved to carry the precious limestone cargo across the Bristol Channel. They were rigged as Poleacres or 'muffrodite' (Derr. Hermaphrodites) – a mixture of brigantine and schooner, sturdy and buoyant, yet graceful – they must have made a lovely picture.

Mr John Chugg, who had been an assistant Master at the Barnstaple Blue Coat School in the 1930's had been able to interview various lime captains and "Grand old men of the sea, heroes of my youth and friends of my mature years". From one old sea dog he was given the following poem. I quote it, because for me, it not only brings alive the scene from my painting, but also shows us the pride those little vessels evoked in the hardy race of seamen who sailed them.

"Broad in the beam, that the stress of the blast,
Pressing down upon sail and mast,
Might not the sharp bows overwhelm
Broad in the beam, not sloping aft
With graceful curve and slow degrees
That she might be docile to the helm,
And that the currents of parted seas,
Closing behind, with mighty force,
Might aid and not impede her course."

Even the names of these old stone-hackers have a romantic ring: *Elizabeth, Little Jane (from Lynmouth), St. Brannock, Kitty Ann, Alexandra, Magnet, Newton (captured from the French), Emily, Swan (the last of the Muffies), Two Sisters (actually built for Mr Chugg's grandfather in 1865), Ebenezer.*

Records of all these ships are in the Maritime Museum at Barnstaple. We know that they were Torridge built craft; that they were strong, able to carry anything between 70 and 90 tons of limestone in one journey. Many of them, peculiar to North Devon, were unusual in that they could be sailed backwards in order to negotiate the treacherous Bideford Bar (made

The 'Ebenezer' at Clovelly, c.1870.

famous by Kingsley). We can even discover the names of their captains; but unfortunately no records exist of individual journeys or their cargoes.

I had long wondered who had actually owned these boats. The answer to this question came shortly after my arrival in Devon. I was fortunate enough to interview Mr John Travis, who had just published his excellent book, "An Illustrated History of Lynton and Lynmouth". He told me that most of the boats operating out of Lynmouth were held in shares by the Lord of the Manor. In Lynmouth, the Lock and Roe families had emerged as owning the bigger portion of the shares; others were held by several local business men . The boats themselves were multi-purpose vessels, going across the Channel sometimes for a load of limestone, other times for a load of coal. Without doubt some of these boats made their way into Pwlldu Bay .

The 'muffies' were manned by as hardy a race of sailors as ever sailed the Channel. The Shipping Records of 1856-7 give us some idea of how treacherous these waters were. In this year alone there were 87 marine casualties in the Bristol Channel, involving the loss of 114 lives. Not only the treacherous sea, but the effects of wind, or indeed the lack of it, contributed to the hazardous journey. In a Report of the Commissioners on Harbours of Refuge in 1858, a certain Captain Joshua Williams, stated that he had frequently seen as many as 300 vessels, windbound in Swansea. David Jenkins of Pwlldu has reported that often, if the weather turned nasty, ships would stay in the bay until conditions improved. This would explain why Beaufort needed at times to supply accommodation for these stranded sailors.

There is a report that some boats loaded with the heavy limestone, were unable to float off on the next tide, and remained with their cargo on the beach where they quickly became wrecks. In Pwlldu, for many years, the outline of one such wreck, together with its cargo of stone, was regularly revealed at low tide in the Needles Bay. There have been no recent sightings, as no doubt the level of sand has changed over the centuries.

Limestone traders, on arrival at their destination, would turn round on the next tide making between two and sometimes three double voyages in a week. If the weather was particularly good the double journey might be completed in a day. The season ran through Spring, Summer and Autumn (roughly March to November). The *North Devon Journal* of the time gives us many examples of these incredible journeys. Two from the year 1828, are worth quoting:

> *". . . two of the vessels built for the service of Lord Rolle's Canal . . . made each four voyages from Bideford to Wales and returned and discharged their cargoes in one week."*

> *"Captain Guy of Appleford on his brigandine 'Mars' carried four cargoes in five days from S. Wales to Greencleave limekilns, Abbotsham."*

The hardy sailors who sailed these vessels were paid the princely sum of ten to twelve shillings per voyage.

Return Journey to Devon

In the same way as Pwlldu folk had joyously greeted the North Devon 'muffies', their welcome on the other side of the Channel was no less enthusiastic. From a convenient hill, the vessels would be sighted coming down Channel. The skilled crew would perfectly judge the manoeuvres necessary to negotiate the awkward little harbours of North Devon or land onto open beach (such as Heddon's Mouth, near Lynmouth).

In the archives of the Barnstaple Museum was a personal account written by Miss Jane Forbes Wilcocks whose grandfather, Stephen Wilcocks, was once Mayor of Bideford in 1815. Jane recalls how as a child,

> *"I used to stand out on rocks and hail the smacks and polackers when they came home with limestone for the kiln."*

The boats would be run onto the beaches on the top of the tide which saved waiting for the next tide before sailing again. The vessel often came in stern inwards, after letting go of the anchor outside the bay to enable her to 'haul off'.

Two 'Muffies' beached at Combe Martin.

Unloading the 'Emily' at Combe Martin.

The stones would then be unloaded as quickly as possible. Sometimes they would be just pitched overboard at high water. At other times sloping planks would be placed on board, down which the stone would be slid. In the same way as families and groups of men and women in Pwlldu had formed loading gangs responsible for bringing the limestone to the beach and on to the vessels, their counterparts in Devon formed 'discharging gangs' that were responsible for relieving the vessels of their cargo in double quick time. The gangs of 'stone heavers' were made up of casual labourers, men and women. North Devon women, always a source of cheap labour, like their 'sisters' across the water, were given equally back-breaking work. They were expected to heave the heavy stones onto the sands, and then onto the horse drawn butts (carts) to be taken to the lime kilns. Some of the stone was carried in 'Lyme Potts' which were slung from each side of the saddle on the pack horses. Sometimes they would transfer the stone onto river barges, ready to be taken up the Rolle Canal.

It is said that this special breed of women could outswear and outdrink their male companions! In the Census of 1851, their occupation is listed as 'Limestone porter'. While examining back copies of the *North Devon Journal* in the Archives at Appledore, a gentleman approached me. He had overheard my conversation with the Curator and felt he could perhaps interest me in some archive material he had come across. It seemed he was in Appledore searching for details of his own family who had lived in the area during the eighteenth and nineteenth century. One of the fascinating documents he had come across was the report of a court case, held on Thursday 5th September 1850, which concerned his great, great Grandmother, one Elizabeth Toones. She had brought to court a complaint of an assault against her, by a male stone heaver. The dispute had taken place at Appledore when two women had been part of a gang discharging a cargo of limestone. As the quarrel became heated, the husband of one of the women had interfered, giving Elizabeth Toones a violent blow to the head and then proceeding to kick her as she lay on the ground. The magistrates duly found him guilty of a violent assault and he was fined five pounds and sent to the county gaol for two calendar months. One of the magistrates admonished the defendant against striking a woman, to which he coolly replied 'She is not a woman'. This remark implies that female stone heavers, were indeed 'a race apart'!

Much of the imported limestone was landed directly at the

many kilns that had been built to serve the agricultural areas of the hinterland. There were at one time more than a hundred such kilns, although not all were in use at the same time. In 1845, an amazing 90,000 tons was reported to have entered the Taw/Torridge estuary.

The kilns often stood on the banks of tidal rivers and creeks, or were located just above the tide-line of the many little beaches of the rock bound North Devon coast.

John Travis was again able to give me some fascinating details about the kilns and the local politics that were involved in their running. It soon became clear that we were talking of a far more complex industry than the lime quarrying of Pwlldu. Indeed, as the limestone made its journey across the Channel more and more people became involved, huge profits were made, and mostly by the Devon Lords of the Manor. These men not only owned large shares in the boats, but set out to have a monopoly of the whole lime trade. Anyone else bringing in limestone or coal was charged a keelage fee. As early as 1830, a table of tolls was set up on the Rhenish tower of Lynmouth Harbour. As Lords of the Manor, they claimed that this was their right; and after all wasn't it their money that paid for the upkeep and improvements of the harbour? Although this was deeply resented by their tenants, there was little they could do about it unless they wished to lose their tenancy. Thus the Lords of the Manor quickly became the 'Kings' of the Lime Industry, as they were able to sell their lime more cheaply than any of their competitors.

I also found that this monopoly of the trade was not always just achieved by the Lords of the Manor. When examining documents pertaining to Combe Martin, it seemed that here no fewer than five lime burners had banded together in order to 'fix' prices. The Knight family had reclaimed thousands of acres of Exmoor and a vast quantity of lime was needed to work this quite difficult land. They had to bargain with the lime burners of Combe Martin to get a good price. In the 1820's and 30's they were paying 20 shillings a ton for lime and employed three carters and their teams to continuously fetch lime from the kiln.

The limestone kiln at Clovelly behind a forest of masts.
The limestone can be seen on top of the kiln.

Lime Burning

The journey to kilns, could be as much as 14 or 15 miles, although many of the kilns were sited immediately behind the beaches. As they were built above ground level the limestone and culm had to be fed into the 'mouth' of the kiln. Up these quite steep ramps, limestone was carried in a horse drawn cart.

Once again, extracts from the archive material in Bideford Museum, furnished me with the most graphic descriptions of this remarkable industry. None more so than this rather gruesome account by a Mr Jack Richards, who worked as a Carter in the 1850's. He tells us of:

> *". . . a certain old horse and cart that used to take the limestone up the ramp. At the top it was tipped in a heap beside the kiln mouth. The old horse knew his job – up, tip, turn,*

> *down and load again. 'Poor old horse!' – he was an old worn out farm horse – past work, so he'd come to this, so feeble that he fell dead into the kiln and got roasted!"*

Another interesting piece of information he gives us is that often the larger rocks, that could weigh as much as one and a half hundred weight, had to be broken up with sledge hammers into stones, with an average diameter of eight inches, before they could be used in the kiln.

His dramatic account of lime-burning is far more immediate than any text book description:

> *"The fire was kindled from the eye – first brushwood, then faggots, then culm. When the culm fire was thoroughly hot, limestone was thrown down, a stone at a time on to it. When this got hot, another course of culm and stone – each about one foot thick. At last the kiln would be filled up and then all glowing! The fire would die out b'now and be alive at the top.*
>
> *As the lowest part died, it cobbled and contracted, so that the lime caved down and fell. It was now pouring out of the eye and needed little raking out, it was shovelled into the cart."*

This method of lime burning was known as the intermittent method, and the kiln was usually emptied after one week and the process started all over again. The early kilns in Pwlldu, although much smaller, used the same method of burning, as did the kilns in the rest of Gower. Later the 'Continuous Method' was introduced. The loading of the limestone and culm, was exactly the same, but when the lime nearest the fire was raked out, more limestone was added. The kilns were kept burning as long as there was a demand, sometimes for months on end. Once this method became common, the kilns were more strongly constructed, some even brick lined, such as those at Clovelly and Tor Bay. This is why some of the ruins are still intact, both in Gower and Devon.

In the same way that quarrying in Pwlldu tended to run in

families, so too did the highly skilled trade of lime burning. Trade secrets were closely guarded and handed down through the generations. The Jenkins and Jones families of Pwlldu had to know the exact amount of gunpowder to use for blasting and how to gauge the size of stone needed by the lime-burners. Likewise, the quarries and lime kilns of Combe Martin remained in the hands of the Thomas and Cutliffe families who knew the exact temperature that the kiln fire had to be kept in order to ensure that the limestone was not over or underburnt.

In the middle and later decades of the nineteenth century, lime-carts were by far the most common traffic on Exmoor lanes. The Carters, as they were known, were the counterparts of the Pwlldu agricultural labourers who augmented their meagre incomes by working in the quarry and loading the boats. In North Devon most farmers would keep at least one of their labourers and a cart simply to make a round journey every day, or in summer twice a day. These carters were only able to use pack horses or small two wheeled carts on the steep, narrow and often overgrown lanes. At certain times of the year, mainly in the Autumn and Spring, strings of lime laden pack horses became something of a hazard in the district. It was common to find queues of carts and pack horses waiting in the lanes leading to the kilns. Carriers and farmers would wait all night in order to get an early load of lime the following day.

Mr Tithecott, who worked for years as a carter or carrier, describes how he used to come from Bideford in a farm cart for lime –

> *"We'd leave home before three and get there about six. Other carts would arrive before us . . . so if there was a cart there already, we'd sometimes have to come back to Bideford . . ." There was no measuring or weighing, the lime 'all hot' – and 'look out' – for if it rained your cart could be burnt . . . the lime lay in a great bulk in the cart. The man in charge was called the 'lime burner' – he decided just how much was a 'cart load' and the cost."*

By an amusing co-incidence a Mr Richards worked at a farm

known as Beaufort. He tells us that *"farm horses worked three days a week with a day's rest between journeys."*

The grandson of another carter who used to take lime from the kilns at Porlock to farms near North Molton, tells us that his grand-father often made two journeys in one day and then rested the horses on the next:

> *"He began his trips on a Monday, but that meant setting out before midnight on Sunday. He knew the neighbours would be shocked, so he and the other carters used to muffle the wheels of the carts with sacks, until they were well clear of the village."*

It is from archive material such as this that the most accurate information can be gleaned, as written records of the lime industry are not generally available until late in the nineteenth century when the industry was coming to an end. Indeed the only records that appear in the local press of the time are when accidents occur and are sufficiently newsworthy to be reported.

I found some rather gruesome accounts of such accidents in past copies of the *North Devon Journal*. One of the earliest incidents recorded was from the year 1827, when a quarry accident resulted in the death of two men, leaving behind six orphaned children. The deaths had been caused by falling stones during a blasting operation. A similar accident is reported in *The Cambrian* of 1811, when two Pwlldy men also lost their lives.

Another incident that took place in one of the Combe Martin kilns led to the horrific death of Mr Norman, the lime-burner. While making a hole in the top 'crust' of the burning limestone in order to drop down a further load of stone, he fell into the kiln. His screams quickly brought rescuers who managed to get him out. The poor man was then given vast quantities of alcohol to relieve his pain. Now, thoroughly drunk, he was transported away on a hand-cart. His drunken voice could be heard singing "nearer my God to thee". He died a few days later.

Another very poignant incident from Combe Martin was

the death of a young son of the kiln owner. Aged only eight, he fell to his death in the same way as Mr Norman.

The *North Devon Journal* also reports the deaths of many tramps, who having sought out the warmth of the kilns in order to have a good night's rest, often fell into the mouth of the kiln and died an agonising death.

In spite of the many dangers and the hard life led by all the workers connected to the Lime Burning Industry, both in Pwll-du and the small villages and towns of North Devon, we get a picture of men and women, who partly through their grinding work schedules, formed a closely knit community, who knew how to enjoy themselves when the few occasions presented themselves.

In Pwlldu, the quarrymen, the men and women stone heavers, farm workers, fishermen, mariners and lime captains would gather round the bars in Beaufort and The Ship. Alf Jenkins' grandfather had often told of the games of cards that went on in the old Malt House, sometimes throughout the whole night! Gambling was part of the scene, and it is on one such occasion, when the Malthouse itself was put up as a stake that the Jenkins family lost this precious building to the Jones family! To this day it remains part of the Beaufort property.

Across the sea, on the days that the kilns were working, they became the meeting place for all the locals. A great number of people could be gathered there: carters waiting patiently, often in a long queue for their butts to be filled, lime burners tending the kiln, and sometimes lime captains who had just discharged their stones, not to mention the many stone heavers and lime porters. Devon folk tended to prefer jars of cider to pints of ale, and these were freely available. Many of the men and women would take advantage of the hot stones to fry up their bacon and 'butties'.

Devon archives record a number of 'lime feasts' which were held at the end of every season. This event, however, was not for the manual workers, but rather an occasion where hundreds of customers, farmers and market gardeners would get together in a local hotel to talk about the advantages of their precious 'lime manure' and probably where the best price for lime could be attained.

In the 1880's liming had nearly come to a halt. There had been a series of bad harvests, swamping of the meat markets with frozen beef and mutton from overseas; and no longer was there a flourishing local cloth trade requiring wool. With the decline in agriculture few farmers could afford lime for more than their immediate household needs. Old and new pastures were starved and could feed less stock. The importation of cheap food in the second half of the nineteenth century led to a decline in home production. All these factors together with the introduction of artificial manures, signalled a new era in agriculture and the inevitable decline of the lime-burning industry. The limestone quarries were no longer a viable concern and gradually ceased to be worked. The 'Pwlldy' quarry closed by the end of Queen Victoria's reign.

This also had a great effect on the people engaged in the transportation of the limestone and culm. A large number of small coasting vessels formerly used for carrying limestone were laid up in the estuary, as were the larger culm boats.

A visitor to Devon would find that many kilns are still to be seen. In Clovelly the old kiln is still in sound condition and used today for storing equipment used by the fisherman, such

The kiln at Lee Bay now serves as the foundation of a house.
The door on the right hides a delightful chapel.

Top of brick lined kiln at Clovelly 1995.

Heddon's Mouth kiln.

The author waiting for the cliff railway at Lynmouth.

as lobster pots, nets and ropes. The National Trust is now turning its attention to the preservation of some of the more important lime kilns. In Heddon's Mouth, the reconstruction is complete, while in Waters Meet near Lynmouth, work is in hand to do the same to the two kilns found here. In Lynmouth town itself, by some miraculous chance, the old lime kiln which is situated at the foot of the famous Cliff Railway has remained largely intact, and today is used as a shelter, its top being incorporated into a charming patio area, part of public gardens. It is satisfying that these symbols of another age have been incorporated into modern life.

In Pwlldu, more and more tourists were finding the area. When George Jones died in 1887, *The Cambrian* noted that "He was well-known to tourists throughout the area."

Homes and Families in the Valley

Today, as one takes the steep stony path that leads from the top of the cliff on the Bishopston side of the bay, it almost seems as if the road leads directly into the sea; the cove of Pwlldu is temporally out of sight. Then as one rounds the second bend, the full splendour of the bay is revealed: the wide sandy beach, with its distinctive ridge of rounded pebbles, the stream meandering its twisting path to the sea, and nestling directly under the cliff stand the two white houses. Most people are surprised to find any human habitation in such a seemingly isolated spot. Hardly any are aware that at one time there was a third dwelling in the Bay.

Rachel's Cottage

Where the end of the cliff path goes into almost a tunnel of greenery, and just as the first trees of Pwldy Wood appear on the right, immediately bordering the path, one can just make out the ruins of a stone wall. Today these ruins are known as Rachel's Cottage and a local superstition has grown up that everyone who passes the cottage at night must give the greeting, "Good-night Rachel". Rachel was Rachel Timothy who came as a young bride with her husband, John Timothy, to Pwldy about the year 1812. The cottage then was known as 'Pwldy Cottage'.

We know that John Timothy had been born in Llandeilo-Tal-y-bont in the year 1793. He had been brought up in the Pontarddulais district and it is thought that he might well have had some experience of quarrying in this area. We have seen that the limestone trade of Pwldy, by this time was a well established industry, and there is little doubt that he sought employment at the quarry. Fortunately a very early photograph

'Rachel's Cottage': home of John and Rachel Timothy 1873.

A young lady posed in front of the Cottage.

(1873) of the cottage has survived, and we can see what a delightful dwelling it must have been. With its thatched roof, tiny windows and single chimney, it could have come straight out of a 'Hansel and Gretel' story.

The garden was situated opposite the cottage on the sea side of the road, dropping down to the banks of the river. It was quite a sizeable plot and very well managed, providing an abundance of vegetables and fruit for the Timothy family. Indeed, long after the cottage was deserted and fallen into disrepair, the garden was often raided by the Hunts and Jones boys of the neighbouring farms. Here at the turn of the century they could still sample raspberries, gooseberries and currants; and apparently some lovely flowering shrubs continued to flourish. By the 1930's and 40's, when I lived in Pwlldu, nature had overtaken the plot, but you could still find clumps of white violets growing in the one-time garden. Alas today, all traces of the garden have disappeared, and only part of a wall and chimney remain of the cottage.

John Timothy married Rachel, who we know was from the Pennard area. There were two sons, and two daughters of the marriage. The eldest son, John Timothy (Jun) wrote a diary for the first four months of the year 1864, and by incredible chance, the diary has survived, together with a notebook which he had written ten years earlier. Both documents provide a fascinating insight into the social life of these times.

The first detailed Census Returns of 1841, when John Timothy (Jun) was 8 years of age, record his father's occupation as an agricultural labourer. Like most of his neighbours in the valley, this would have been his major occupation; but no doubt he would also have been employed as a 'stone-breaker' in the quarry, with possibly some oyster fishing in the winter, not to mention some smuggling 'on the side'!

In the 1848 Tithe Assessments of Bishopston we can see that apart from his House and Garden (947), he also had a Meadow (941), known as 'The Quarters' or 'Timothy's Meadow', together with 'Timothy's Close' – arable (942) and Pwldy Wood (943).

Rachel Timothy died in 1854, and by the 1861 Census, John Timothy (Sen) was living with his daughter Rachel and son,

John, the other children having left home. Although the name of John Timothy (Jun) appears on the Census Form, we know from his surviving notebook that he was by this time lodging in Oystermouth (at least for a period in Park Street, which was then newly built). By now John's main occupation was oyster-dredging, but like his father he still found work in the quarry, probably Clement's Quarry, Oystermouth, or sometimes in the Pwldye quarry. From May until August, when the oysters were out-of-season, he would have helped in the local farms of Bishopston or High Pennard. Before his marriage, although lodging in Mumbles, he still considered the cottage at Pwlldu as 'home', and he returned there most weekends, and indeed at other times when he was needed to help out with work in the garden and fields. It is the accounts of such visits that I have found so valuable in unravelling the social life of Pwlldy during the early 19th century.

The 1871 Census gives John Timothy (Sen) as living alone with his unmarried daughter, Rachel, whose age is given as 40. By the end of the year, John Timothy (Sen) dies, and it is possible that Rachel lived on in Pwlldu for a short time, but by the 1891 Census there is no record of occupancy at the cottage. A local story has been told of a piece of burning furze pushed down the chimney which in turn set the roof alight. I have been unable to find any evidence to support this story and am more inclined to believe that the cottage just fell into ruins.

John Timothy (Jun) was quite an exceptional character. In 1854 he was attending 'a day school at night', in order to improve his education. Not only enterprising, but thrifty as well, he regularly paid into an early type of 'Building Society' in Mumbles. In 1865 he married Mary Davies, whose father was a blacksmith in Wellington Street, Swansea. A year after his marriage, in December 1866, he was able to purchase a building plot on land known as 'the two acres' – which became Gloucester Place, Oystermouth. A small four-roomed traditional cottage was soon built to house the rapidly increasing family – eight children in all! The children all survived and made good marriages. Even today the same cottage is lived in by one of John Timothy's direct descendants, and I am assured that the large 'Timothy' family of today often assemble together at Christmas and other occasions and fill the small cottage with joy and celebrations – so one might say that 'Rachel's Cottage' in one sense is still alive!

Pooldie House (later known as 'Ship')
home of the Jenkin family

Limestone quarrying, as we have seen, is thirsty work in any century, so it is not unreasonable to assume that there was an Inn at Pwlldu as early as the seventeenth century and perhaps even earlier. The 1803 Duke of Beaufort's Estate Map shows the cottage and a smaller building opposite which is the Malt House. At a later date the bakehouse built by John Jenkin was to become part of the new Beaufort Inn.

What makes this house and its history so interesting is that the Jenkin family kept it for at least two hundred years. They are inextricably bound up with the very fabric of the history of Pwlldu during the years 1700-1970 and as their direct descendants continued to live in The Ship, one could expect the oral memory to be more accurate than usual.

The first written evidence of a John Jenkin living in 'Pouldie' is in 1732 when there is a faint signature in the Pennard Parish Register by a John Jenkin. Unfortunately there is only a fragment of the page left and it is difficult to make out anything other than the name, date and place. It is very probably the recording of a birth, as the death of a John Jenkin is recorded in 1813, and his age is given as 81; this fits in perfectly with this earlier birth date.

The Land Tax Payments of the year 1766 record that 'pooldie House and land' has Thomas Popkin as the Landlord and Moses David is named as the undertenant. This could well be the man who was first involved in building the road down the cliff from Bishopston, as the road became known as Moses Road, and even today this is the name given to it by older residents. By

1775 and the immediate succeeding years, John Jenkin is listed as the undertenant, while the Duke of Beaufort is the Landlord.

As early as 1786 'Pooldie House' was selling beer. For the three years ending at Michaelmas 1789, a John Jenkin is listed as paying his 'toll piece' of one shilling to the Duke of Beaufort, 'for selling ale'.

Two faint marriage entries, for Dec. 1763 and 1766, record the marriage of a John Jenkin, first to Bridget Jenkin and then three years later to an Elizabeth Bevan. Whether Bridget died

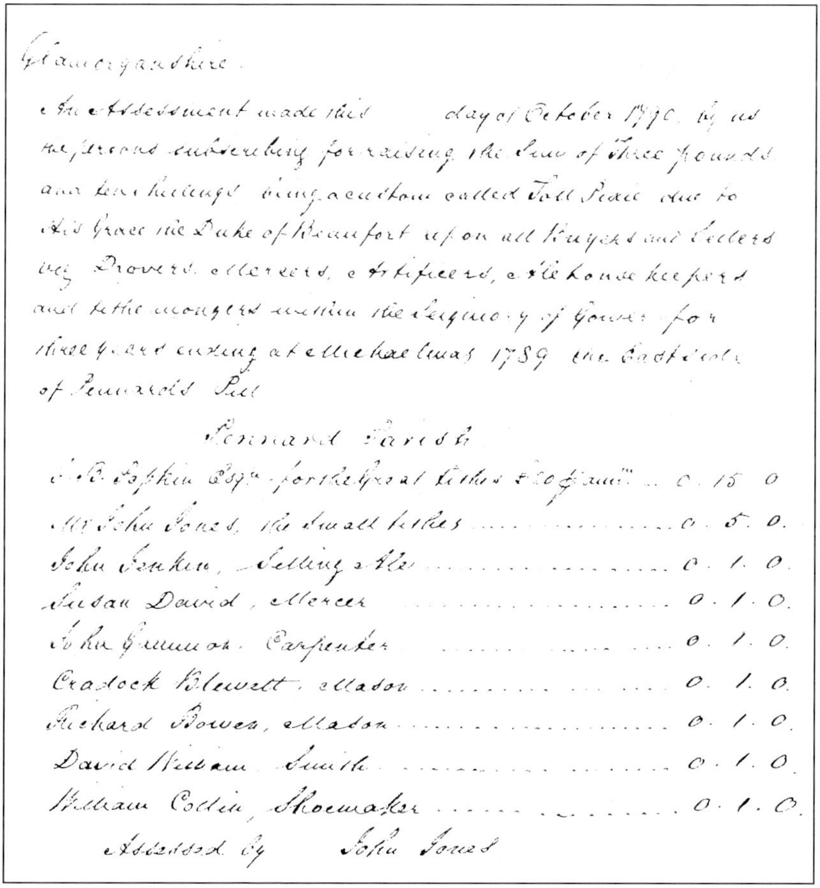
Glamorganshire.

An Assessment made this day of October 1790 by us the persons subscribing for raising the Sum of Three pounds and ten shillings being a custom called Toll Piece due to His Grace the Duke of Beaufort upon all Buyers and Sellers viz Drovers, Mercers, Artificers, Ale house keepers and tithe mongers within the Seigniory of Gower for three years ending at Michaelmas 1789 the Eastside of Pennard's Peel

Pennard Parish

[illegible] Popkin Esqr. for the Great tithes & 20 of ann[illegible]	0. 15. 0
Mr John Jones, the small tithes	0. 5. 0.
John Jenkin, Selling Ale	0. 1. 0.
Susan David, Mercer	0. 1. 0.
John Gammon, Carpenter	0. 1. 0.
Cradock Blewett, Mason	0. 1. 0.
Richard Bowen, Mason	0. 1. 0.
David Williams Smith	0. 1. 0.
William Collin, Shoemaker	0. 1. 0.

Assessed by John Jones

Part of an Assessment for raising the sum of three pounds and ten shillings called 'The Toll Piece' due to His Grace, the Duke of Beaufort – Oct. 1790.

or whether there are two men with the name of John Jenkin, we can only surmise – what we do know is that John and Elizabeth Jenkin set up house in Pouldie; indeed Elizabeth lived there to the remarkable age of 89 and her husband also reached the considerable age of 81. It would seem from the longevity of these two lives that if one survived the dangers of birth and early childhood, the healthy air of Pwlldu could lead to a long life!

Unfortunately the history of the young family started by the couple two years after their marriage was not to be so happy. Two sons were born, John and David. These were probably twins as their baptisms and deaths are recorded just sixteen days apart in December of 1768. The following year a daughter, Elizabeth, is born, but she was to live for only fifteen years. A second daughter, Ann, was born in 1775.

Then in 1800 John Jenkin married a Elizabeth Tucker, who came from the Tucker family in Reynoldston There were no fewer than nine children born between 1805-1826. On all these entries John Jenkin is described as an Innkeeper. When one realises that the Ship Inn at this time was a modest Gower cottage with just two bedrooms the question arises – 'Where did they all sleep?' Obviously the family had not only to share rooms but beds as well – three to a bed was quite common, and a partition was often placed down the middle of the room to separate the sexes. If anyone had an infectious disease then it was likely to spread very quickly through the family.

Fortunately all of the children seemed to survive childhood, and indeed with the exception of one son, John, who died when he was twenty, all lived to make successful marriages.

By examining the Parish records and the Census Returns some very interesting information is revealed. As one would expect, these marriages were either to members of families living in High Pennard, less than half a mile away, or to farming families from the immediate area, and this was to be the pattern for the next fifty years or more. It is little wonder that this was such a closely knit community where everyone helped everyone else – after all most of them were related by marriage in some way or other!

A lobster fisherman, thought to be David Jenkins, in Needles Bay, Pwlldu – C. E. Schenk, August 1886.

Cliff Cottage – Gertrude Rees, 1959.

The Beaufort

Between the year 1830 and the year 1840 a second Inn had been built in the valley, to serve the large numbers of men and women involved in the Limestone trade which was beginning to reach its peak. The exact date when the inn was built is very difficult to pinpoint, but there are intriguing parts of the historical jig-saw that might help us. Quite by chance, while sifting through the Parish records of Bishopston, among the birth entries I came across the birth of a daughter, Caroline, to George and Hannah Bluet; the family is living in Pwldy. The father's occupation is given as a mason. No such name appears in the 1841 Census of either of the houses in Pwlldu. The Jenkins family are living in Ship so there is just a possibility that this young mason has been employed to build the new inn.

The very first deed for Beaufort is in 1840. The house and garden is part of the 'Lunnon lands' which form part of the Kilvrough Estate (989 acres in all, covering Pennard, Bishopston, Ilston, Llanridian (Higher and Lower). The deed is drawn up between Thomas Penrice and Anne Griffiths. The lease is for 99 years from April 30th 1840, and the rent is £4 per annum.

In 1841 we have the most interesting Census Returns. For the first time details of the family, together with their ages and place of abode are given. One of the families living in Poolday is a married couple – John and Elizabeth Rosser. The only other member of the household is Elizabeth Phillip 15, who is classed as 'Independent' and is possibly from the Phillip family living in one of the cottages of High Pennard. It is almost certain that these people are the first occupants of Beaufort.

Births, Deaths and Marriages in the two Inns

It is easy to be more certain of the occupants of Ship. The Jenkin family is still there. John Jenkin, head of the household, now 65 years of age, is living with his three sons: George and David, (both 20), and young Hezekiah (15). His wife, Elizabeth had died in 1832.

LANDOWNERS	OCCUPIERS	Numbers referring to the Plan	NAME AND DESCRIPTION of LANDS AND PREMISES	QUANTITIES in STATUTE MEASURE a.	r.	p.	PAYABLE TO Vicar £	s.	d.	PAYABLE TO Impropriator £	s.	d.
			Pwldye Village									
Beaufort Duke of	Samuel Jones	493	Public House	-	-	20			2	-	-	2
	John Jenkins	494	Public House and Garden		1	18			7			11

Part of document listing 'Tithe Apportionment of 1846'.

Two important marriages were to take place from the Valley in 1843. The first marriage indicates that the Jones family, originally from Bishopston, were now resident at Beaufort and this family was to stay in the inn until the turn of the

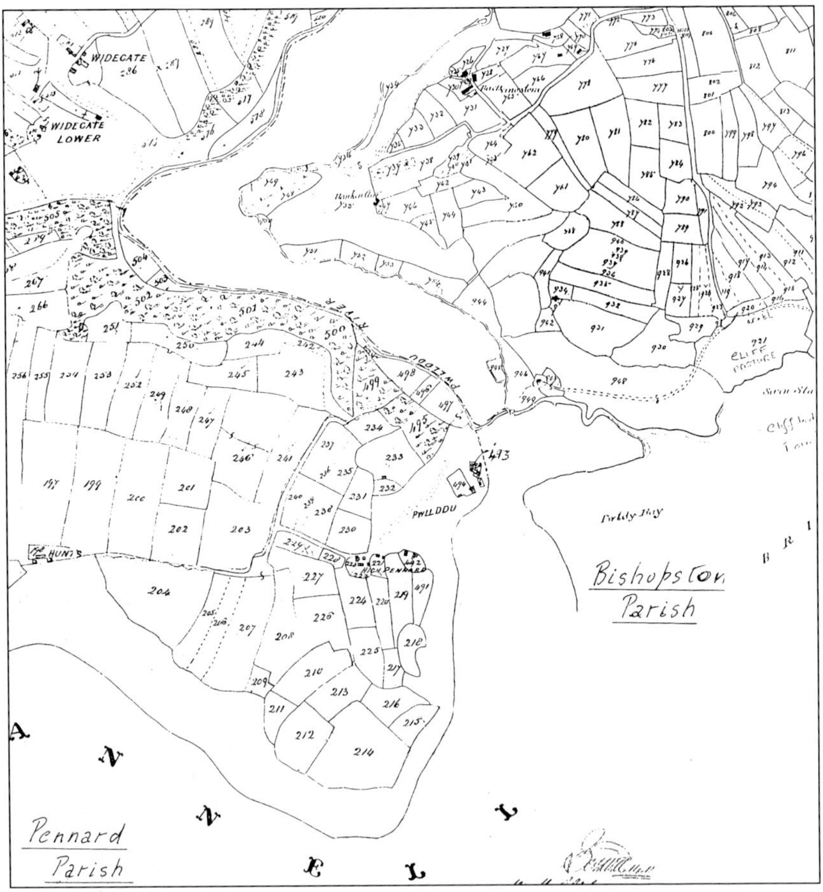

Tithe Apportionment Map with field names.

SOME INTERESTING ENTRIES IN THE TITHE APPORTIONMENT OF 1848

No.	*Property (Field names)*	*Owner*	*Tenant*
HIGH PENNARD			
222	House and garden (arable)		John Lloyd
229	Croft		
492	High Pennard House (later Cliff Cottage)		William Davies
217, 219, 220, 230, 231 – farmed by William Davies			
208	Body Acre		
209	Body Acre Homestead		Gwenllwyn Jones
212	The Wall		
246	Merchants Close		Samuel Jones
LAND IN THE VALLEY			
930	The Three Acres	David Edwards	Samuel Jones
931	Cliffland in Great Close		John Jenkins
920, 921, 922	Cliffland or Cardigan		
944, 945, 946	Pwldy Meadow	Eaton Roberts	John Davies
941	The Quarters		John Timothy
942	Timothy's Close		
943	Pwldy Wood		
947	House and garden		
949	Part of Pwldwy Beach	Duke of Beaufort	
929	Butter Close (arable)	John Griffiths	
747	House and garden Hanken Cliff		
746	Field by the house		
742	Pool Path Field		
741	Landshare in Quartere (with 739,740 site of Paradise Meadow)		
744	Cold Rhydings		
755	Hanken Cliff	COMMONS	

century. Samuel Jones's eldest son, another Samuel Jones, was married to Irene Davies, the daughter of Isaac Davies (deceased) of Great Kittle Farm. Samuel Jones is described as a Farmer; and young Samuel as a 'Farmer's Son' (an important social distinction from an agricultural Labourer). There is no doubt that this 'Farmer's Son' had made a very advantageous marriage as Great Kittle Farm was one of the largest in the area.

The second marriage of this year was between David Jenkin of 'Pooldie' and Mary Lloyd of High Pennard. Mary's father, John Lloyd, farmed a few acres, and lived in one of the larger cottages in High Pennard (see Tithe Apportionment Map. Nos 222 and 229). There were two other children in the family, also a young servant girl who had come from Oxwich.

After their marriage, the young couple (David was 29 and Mary 22) lived in High Pennard. Whether they had their own cottage is not certain, but we do know that their first four children: Elizabeth, Jane, William and David were all born in High Pennard. It is significant that David's occupation on the Birth Entries is given as a Farmer. It could be that he was helping his father and/or his father-in-law.

Another infant death is recorded in Pwldy in 1845. This is the tragic death of Elizabeth Jones just 11 weeks old.

Among the earliest records of both inns is the 'Tithe Apportionment of 1846'. This document amusingly refers to the two buildings as Pwldye Village. Neither inn is given a name; both are referred to as Public Houses one of which has a garden. Samuel Jones and his family are now occupying Beaufort. He is paying 2d to his landlord – the Duke of Beaufort, and 2d for the vicar.

In 1848 we have the first indication of the strong ties that are to link the two houses over the next fifty years. A glance at the Tithe Apportionment map shows that Samuel Jones jointly farms with John Jenkin of Ship several acreages near their homesteads: nos. 930, 931 – Cliffland in Great Close; 921 – Cliff – pasture; 922 – small piece of arable land (see map).

The 1851 Census continues the story. Samuel Jones (aged 38) and his wife Jane (35) have three sons: Thomas (3), Robert (2), and baby David (10 months). The other member of the household is Mary Lloyd, the first of many servant girls to work at this busy pub.

There has also been a significant change in Ship. The Head of the household is Eliza Davies, who had married in 1836. Her husband now dead, she has returned to her family home at Ship bringing her two young daughters, Elizabeth (5) and Jane (11). Living with them are her brother, George Jenkins, and nephew James Jenkins (24), who is described as a mariner.

Between 1851 and 1852, there must have been quite an upheaval in the valley. All the previous occupants of Ship move out. In a few years George was to marry Anne Eaton (1860) and perhaps James moved to Swansea. A direct descendent, Peter Thomas, (now living in Pennard), believes that his great

James Jenkins, living in 'Ship' 1851.

grandfather James became a Swansea pilot. I have not been able to trace where Eliza and her daughters went.

What we do know (Pennard Parish Records) is that a young daughter, Elizabeth, was born to David and Mary in 1852, at Pwldye; so they must have been living in Ship by this time. They have moved down the cliff from High Pennard, together with their four children.

When one remembers that this was the height of the quarrying trade, it could well be that a busy inn was too much for Eliza to run, especially if James leaves for his sea career and George has married.

Then in 1855 from a notice in *The Cambrian* we note that David Jenkins (Victualler) is applying for a license at Ship Inn, Pooldie. This is the first written evidence we have of the name, Ship Inn.

The same year as the new young Jenkins family has moved to Ship, tragedy strikes the Beaufort. In the year 1852, three members of the Jones family were to die, all within two weeks of each other, in the month of December. Husband Sam, and wife Jane, died on December 17th, and four days later, their new baby son, William, just fifteen weeks old, also died. These three deaths would seem to point to some deadly infectious disease, such as small pox, or cholera. Three young sons: Thomas (6), Robert (3), and David (2), are suddenly orphaned. Obviously the other members of the family, who still lived in Bishopston, must have taken them in.

Six children were born to David and Mary Jenkins at Pwll-du. Tragically the pattern of childhood death returns to haunt the Jenkins family. In 1861, William Jenkins, 17 years of age died on October 13th. The same month, just 18 days later, his young sister, only 10 years of age, also died. Before the family had time to recover from these deaths, their young son John, just four years of age, died on September 21st, 1863.

Although there was nothing uncommon about infant death at this time, all these tragic deaths in the valley of Pwlldu in the 1850's and 60's seems to point to a particularly virulent disease. We know that the dreaded disease of cholera visited Swansea during these years, and particularly so in the hamlet of Killay. It could be that this disease had been brought into the valley by the Clyne miners, who apparently often walked down the valley to drink in the Beaufort bar.

On my fact-finding tour of North Devon, the local historian John Travis mentioned that in the 1860's, cholera had been prevalent in Lynton and Lynmouth. There was a strong body of opinion at the time, that the disease might have travelled across the Channel via the Lime-Captains and their crews. So strong was this fear that there was a special meeting of the Local Council to consider whether the 'muffies' should cease trading. The 'Lime-Captains' and indeed the hundreds of people involved in the lime-stone industry were so alarmed at the prospect of their livelihood being taken away from them, that they marched on the Council offices in protest. The threatened trade was allowed to continue.

From the 1861 Census, we learn that George and Susannah Jones from Bishopston have moved into Beaufort. George is described as a Victualler, and no other occupation is given, which implies that like Ship, the inn is kept very busy. Their five children: George (23), Jane (21), Thomas (13), John (10), and Mary (7), are with them. George is a quarryman, while Jane is described as a housemaid. All the children had been born in Bishopston.

After all the tragedies that had occurred in both families in the 1860's it must have been a welcome relief to look forward to some weddings.

In 1860 George Jenkins (age 21), described as a labourer living in Pwlldye, had married Annie Eaton, also aged 21, from Hael Farm – another advantageous alliance for the Jenkins family.

In November 1865, another link took place between a 'daughter of the valley 'and the farming community. This time the wedding was in Beaufort. Young Jane Jones, George Jones's eldest daughter, married William Davies, whose father farmed extensive acreage in High Pennard (see Tithe Map).

A year later, on October 25th, perhaps the most important wedding in the history of Beaufort and Ship, took place. Both inns were now to be linked by marriage, and one can imagine the joy and celebrations that must have ensued. David Jenkins's eldest daughter, Jane, now twenty-three years of age, was married to George Jones's eldest son, also named George, age twenty-eight.

The memory of that day survived down the centuries and Alf Jenkins told me how his father David (Jun), and his grandfather David (Sen), had passed on details of the great rejoicing that took place in both inns.

The 1871 Census shows David and Mary Jenkins, both now aged 50, living with Hezekiah (18), Mary (12), Eliza (8). What is interesting is that David Jenkins (Jun) now 21, has brought his young bride, Matilda, to live at Ship.

Across the way at Beaufort, George and Susannah Jones are living with their sons, Thomas (23), John (20), and Mary (16). All the men in both families are described as 'quarrymen', so the quarry is still in business.

Another piece of the Pwlldu jig-saw is put into place with the marriage in 1875 between John Jones of Pwlldy (24), and Celina Gwynn from Higher Hareslade, Bishopston. The witnesses are John's brother, Thomas Jones from Beaufort, and David Jenkins from Ship. It is noticeable that all parties were able to sign their names. This was a particularly interesting piece of information for me to find, because the grandsons of John Jones of Beaufort are Arthur, Ivor, and David Jones. These three men have been able to give me invaluable help by describing their own lives in Lower Hareslade Farm (situated on the bottom of the cliff just above Brandy Cove), and details of their farming in Pwlldu Bay at the turn of the century. Ivor Jones and his family lived in Knapp farm for many years, and his son, Alan Jones and his family, live in High Pennard farm today. The family's link with Pwlldu has never been broken.

In 1876, young Mary Ann Jones, the youngest child of George and Susannah, marries Robert Lloyd (22), a young police officer. The Lloyd family had lived in a croft in High Pennard for many generations. A glance back at the Tithe Apportionment shows that Robert's grand-father farmed a piece of Pwlldy Meadow together with quite a sizeable Garden and fields nos. 222, 229. In the 1881 Census, John Lloyd is described as a farmer of 4 acres.

By the year 1881 the population of the valley had markedly decreased; indeed the census returns list only five people living in Pwlldye Village. William Jones' brother, George Jones with his wife Jane (née Jenkins) have come to Pwlldu to run Beaufort. In Ship David and Mary Jenkins are living with their 17 year old daughter, Eliza.

The surviving deeds of the house, which state that in 1879 the proprietor of 'Beaufort Arms' (the first written evidence for the public house to carry this name) is William Jones, the acreage is given as .398 and the lease is for 60 years from September 29th. In 1885, the tithe paid is 8 shillings. The Indenture of lease for 1885 still gives William Jones of Bishopston as Maltster, and he is to pay the yearly rate of £8 for 60 years.

The same year, a similar Indenture for Ship, is between the Most Noble Henry Charles Fitzroy, Duke of Beaufort, and David Jenkins of Pwlldu. David Jenkins is described as a quarryman, and this ties in with the information given me by his grand-son, Alfred Jenkins, who told me his grandfather was

John Jones of Pwlldy in later life.

William Jones, Proprietor of Beaufort, 1879.

one of the very last men to work in the quarry. The lease is for 60 years, and the rental is for two half yearly payments of £3 12 shillings.

> *"And the said Lessee, his executors, administrators or assigns shall not nor will use or permit to be used the said primises hereby demised or any part thereof as a Public House or Liquor Shop or Beer shop without the consent of the said Duke, his heirs or assigns in writing under his or their hands."*

There is no record of David Jenkins applying for such permission, and unlike William Jones, he is not referred to as a Maltster; this would imply that from this date Ship ceased to be a public house.

The next ten years were to see very significant changes in the Inns themselves and the people who ran them. Two new family names appear. There was obviously plenty of room in both houses and the new lodgers would help out with the day to day running of the inns. Eliza Jenkins has married Francis Charles, who had come over from Devonshire (possibly on one of the 'muffies'). They go to join Eliza's parents at 'Ship'. In 1889, their baby son, Francis, is born in Pwlldu, followed in 1891 by another son, William Arthur.

It is significant that both David Jenkins, and his son-in-law, are now described as farm labourers, and this very probably was their main occupation. As we know, the quarry is coming to its last days, very few 'muffies' are sailing into the bay. The population is not only decreasing in the valley, but also in High Pennard, where some of the families are moving elsewhere. No longer can they rely on quarrywork to supplement their wages. The original drinking populace had greatly reduced. There is no record of Ship applying for a license after this date, and before long, under the management of Matilda and David Jenkins (Jun), it was to become a Tea-Room and Shop, supplying non-alcoholic drinks, home-made lemonade, and home baking, to the slowly increasing number of tourists who were beginning to find the valley. Indeed from this date the name Ship seems to have been used less and less. People referred to the shop as 'Jenkins' and this name stayed until the late 1970's when the Jenkins family no longer lived in the Valley.

Beaufort continued to be a very busy pub, but the clientele had changed. People were beginning to walk out and 'discover' Gower. It is about this time that the Swansea Art Society had painting expeditions to Gower, and Charles Schenk was a well-known local artist who painted many scenes of the valley from 1870-1907.

Shooting parties from the big houses around, such as Kilvrough and Fairwood, would end their day's sport with a drink at Beaufort and often a meal as well.

It is about this time that Beaufort was extended and the hitherto 'lean to' was converted into a double storied wing onto the main house. There is little doubt that this was built to cater for this new clientele. Not only did it provide a new and bigger bar, leading into a new dining room; but upstairs a fine new 'parlour' was made, complete with the latest cast iron fireplace, a bay window, and even a corniced ceiling. Two extra bedrooms were also available.

Beaufort with new extension, including bay window.

In 1887, George Jones died and the running of Beaufort fell into the capable hands of Jane, his wife.

In the April of 1896, Mary Jenkins, aged 74, died and five years later, her husband David Jenkins (Sen), died at the age of 79. This is when David Jenkins (Jun) and his wife Matilda take over the running of Ship. Their children are born and brought up in the valley: William Hezekiah, Hezekiah John, Walter Edmund, Alfred, and two girls, Selina Jane and Florence. Alfred was to later marry Mary Annie (originally from Llanelli, although living in Swansea). 'Alf' or 'Mr Jinks' as we knew him, is the original narrator of many of my stories of Pwlldu. Mary Annie was to become 'Ma Jenkins of Ship' a character loved and visited by literally hundreds of people and their families who came to discover Pwlldu and enjoy its beauties over the years.

In the 1881 Census Jane Jones is described as 'head' of the Beaufort household. Lodging with her is Walter Sparks, who like his friend, Francis Charles in Ship, originally hailed from Devonshire. In 1886 Walter brings his new bride Ann (father Griffiths Jones of Bishopston). Their first son, Arthur, is born the same year, but dies at only ten weeks old. Another baby son, David James is born in Pwlldu in 1893.

The Jenkins Family, c.1900. Back row, from left: Selina, William Hezekiah, Hezekiah John, Aunt Jane. 2nd row: Matilda, Florence, David. Front: Walter, Alfred.

Aunt Jane, with members of the family outside Beaufort, c.1880.

Among the baptisms recorded in the Pennard Parish records is a son, Arthur, to Alfred and Elizabeth Skinner of Pwlldu, who were living at Beaufort. What is particularly significant, is that even as late as 1889, Alfred is described as a quarryman. It could well be that together with David Jenkins, he was one of the few men employed to close down the quarry. As a child Alf Jenkins had seen the last of the ships in the Bay at about the turn of the century. When the Skinners' second son is born, Alfred has become a groom at Kittle Farm.

In Beaufort Jane Jones had become a much loved Pwlldu character; known as 'Aunt Jane' to one and all, and the fame of her 'suppers' had spread far and wide. In 1907 at the age of 64 her life came to a sudden and tragic end. While visiting a brewery in Swansea in order to settle an account, she fell to her death down a manhole which had been left open. Her funeral attracted many, many people who had known and loved her. Her direct descendent, Mrs Lily Jenkins, who was a young girl of six at the time, could still remember her funeral which was a very grand affair. Apparently the long line of mourners stretched up the whole length of the steep path leading up to Webb's Cottage. The 'funeral road', as it was then called, skirted the fields behind the house, until it reached Widegates. It then made its way up the lane directly to Pennard Church.

The fields belonged to Hunts Farm and Mr Ivor Jones assured me that there would always be someone from Hunts, sitting near the gate where the mourners had to pass. This man claimed 1d for the coffin and mourners to pass through the fields.

A few days before a funeral was due to take place, some of the local farmers would get together to trim back any undergrowth and overhanging branches that might be blocking the funeral road. The heavy coffin would be carried on an equally heavy bier, and the long route to Pennard Church could only be successfully negotiated by groups of farmers taking turns at carrying the coffin.

Most of the people from Beaufort and Ship were buried in Pennard churchyard, because it would have been very difficult to take a coffin up the other side and round the road to Bishopston. The path through the valley would have been equally difficult, as it was not wide enough for a coffin to pass through.

The death of Aunt Jane marked the end of an era in Pwlldu; life in the Valley would never be quite the same again.

Plain Living in Harsh Times

The Landscape

What did the Valley look like at this time? A contemporary account by C. D. Morgan in 1860 makes us realise it was very different from the place we find today:

> *". . . a pretty little cove, quiet asleep at the foot of High Pennard. A high ridge of pebbles fringe the beach, and looking up there is a lovely view of the valley with its green meadows and shady groves. A little brook meanders through the mead ending in a large pool under an overhanging rock, and then finds its way through the pebbles to the shingly strewn sands."*

A later description from George Wade, writing in 1913, tells us that the valley and bay has become,

> *". . . a favourite rendeyvous for Swansea excursionists. It owes its local reputation to the picturesqueness of its valley, which descends tortuously to the sea. It is wild and luxuriant by turns. Outcrops of weathered rock plentifully stud the glen; and its heather clad slopes are here and there variegated with thick patches of woodland. The defile abounds in geological eccentricities and a capricious little streamlet at its bottom continues to lose itself for a while underground. The forsaken bed of the stream furnishes a rough and ready road to the little pebble bay which finally receives its water under the overhanging cliffs of Pwlldu Head."*

The green water meadows are no longer there; the valley has become very overgrown. These meadows had been part of the Pwlldye landscape for many years. We have already noted from the 1848 Tithe Apportionment documents, that these same fields, running directly alongside the river, were jointly farmed by John Jenkin and George Jones.The same fields in the early 1900's were farmed by the same Jones family, who by then were living in Lower Hareslade Farm. They would have been seeded and then the sheep would have been allowed to graze in them, thus keeping back the weeds. The sheep would trample all over the ground, and eat around the hedges, while their feet would break up all the small weeds, even the daisies and buttercups. A good meadow is one where sheep have grazed for years, and this was certainly true, not only of these meadows in the bay, but those that spread right up the valley, on either side of the river. This is the same landscape that I knew as a girl before the beginning of the Second World War.

In C. D. Morgan's description there is no hint of a bridge and it could well be that at this time there were only stepping stones. In his book, *Wanderings in Gower*, Morgan tells an amusing tale of a certain quarryman, name of Will Beynon, possibly the same Will Beynon who owned a Croft and land in Southgate in 1846 – the same Will Beynon who was renowned for his drinking prowess – and obviously a well-known Pwll-du character. His wife, although small, is described as a 'termagant', and used to insist on her husband carrying her over the Pil. Will did not like this; so one day as he waded through the water, when he got to the deepest part he stooped low, and as the water splashed over Betty, she screamed!

> *"Hould thee tongue maid,"* said Will. *"I only want to put thee down, to take thee up better!"*

By 1887 there was a bridge, which was painted by the well-known Swansea artist, Charles Schenk. It was just a plank resting on two stone plinths.

The first known photograph of Pwlldu Village, 1873.
High Pennard House (Cliff Cottage) can be seen at the top of the picture.

The Houses

As we have seen the first written evidence of a house at Pool-die is in the 1766 Land Tax Returns. This building could be an extension of an earlier building. The earliest cottages of the sixteenth century had been replaced in the period referred to as the 'Great Rebuilding' by Elizabethan and later cottages. It is very probable that Ship originally had a thatched roof the same as Pwldye Cottage.

The earliest photograph we have of Pwlldye Village is one taken in June, 1873. This photograph was taken at the same time as the picture of Rachel's Cottage and has remained in the Timothy family. This was just after the time that C. D. Morgan was writing about the bay. The Beaufort has now been built and both cottages are based on the design of a traditional Gower Cottage. The walls, about 22 inches thick, consisted of an inner and outer 'skin' of dressed limestone blocks with a rubble infill. The Ship was a double fronted building with three windows on the top storey, and below, one window on either side of a central doorway. The windows are slightly larger than the normal cottage windows; there seems to be a trace of Georgian influence. The front door opened onto a steep wooden staircase which led to two quite small upstairs bedrooms. Downstairs there were just two rooms, one of which held the traditional large open fireplace, with a thick wooden beam placed immediately above it. The ceilings, of course, were timber beamed, and the upstairs rooms would have been open to the roof. A feature in Ship, Beaufort, and Cliff Cottage was the 'stepped' Gower chimney piece, which extended right through the upper rooms to the roof. Of course, there was the inevitable lean-to containing the scullery and dairy. The floors were 'slabbed' with large rectangular pieces of limestone. In the early days of both Inns these floors would have been sprinkled with sand. The ceiling beams contained large hooks on which whole sides of salted pig were hung.

The Beaufort was built in exactly the same way, but even from the beginning was considerably larger than Ship. It boasted a porch over the front door and the two downstairs rooms were slightly larger, both having broad open fireplaces. The upper windows are slightly smaller than those of Ship, more like those found in Pwldye Cottage and Cliff Cottage. Again there are three windows on the top floor, and one either side of the front door. The central staircase led to two bedrooms, both bigger than those of Ship. Both rooms had the large 'stepped' chimney pieces that extended from the open fireplaces below right through to the roof. Quite a large 'lean-to' was built onto the sea-facing wall and there was another smaller 'lean-to' on its side wall.

It would seem that there was very little garden at this time, and the stones of the beach came almost up to the door. Indeed in an early painting, a prow of a boat can be seen almost up to the boundary wall, seeming to indicate that the tide probably

Beehive oven in the old bakehouse of Beaufort (to left of modern stove).

came much nearer the houses than at present. Beaufort was built on the layers of limestone spoil from the quarry, and the ridges of stone formed by wind and tide gave both houses a natural protection from the ravages of a high tide. All the walls of the houses, both inner and outer, would have a thick layer of limestone wash, which would be replenished at frequent intervals. At the right of the picture is the small bake-house with its distinctive narrow chimney. This is where the 'bee-hive' oven is placed. This building is the very oldest part of Beaufort, having been originally built as a bake-house for John Jenkin. Later it was used by both houses, not only for baking bread but also other Gower specialities. One of these was dowset – a custard tart nearly four inches thick. On sheep washing days, cheese cakes were traditionally supplied to the men as part of their lunch. The ewes milk would be curdled with vinegar, and the curds then flavoured with nutmeg and currants, and enclosed between two layers of pastry on a large slab. Just such a cheesecake was brought down the cliff to the

Jones' boys when they were sheep-washing in the 1930's. Billy Ace, who was married to one of Alf Jenkins's sisters, remembers that slices of dowset, made by Ma Jenkins would always be decorated with a bay leaf picked from the tree that grew in Ship's garden.

The other building in the picture is the old Malt house, which appears on the early Estate map of 1803. It is here that malt would be prepared from barley and distributed to the two inns in Pwlldu, and very possibly to the many farmers in the surrounding area that used it to brew their own beer. Even this small building had been built in exactly the same way. It had its own open fireplace and bee-hive oven. In spite of its size, it had two stories, but the upper floor was little more than a platform, mainly for storage.

The large fire-places did little to relieve the cold in Winter which could be severe. People tended to live on top of the fire, which was fed with wood off the beach. This would be easy for the Jenkins and Jones families, but not so convenient for the cottages and farms high on either cliff. Their fuel, if it was not available from the neighbouring woods, would have to be laboriously carried up from the beach. This was often done with the help of horses and donkeys, the wood being either strapped in a special 'rope' carrier over the back of the animal or dragged behind on the wooden 'slide cars' that were beginning to be used for transporting heavy loads. In the same way bunches of 'smitty sticks' would be collected and carried away. This cheap and easily available fuel was obtained after the furze on the cliff face had been deliberately burnt to allow for new growth, and to provide this much sought after fuel. The burnt furze stumps, known as 'smitty sticks', would be pulled out by hand, often by the women and children, and then carefully stored away for future use as fuel, usually when the bee-hive oven was used for baking.

The cottages would be quite dark even in the daytime, especially during the Winter. Candles often had to be used by day and night, although the large open fires did spread some light. In earlier days rush lights would have been used, often made by women and children. Reeds were readily available from the banks of the Bishopston River. They would be cut into small lengths, the central pith removed, and then successively dipped into mutton fat or tallow, until they were as thick as a small finger. By the nineteenth century, tallow candles were replaced with oil lamps. All the three houses that I knew so well, were lit in this way until at least the 1940's. Indeed I can remember what a great deal of time was spent keeping the oil lamps cleaned, trimmed and filled. One of my earliest memories is my grand-mother placing an oil lamp in the bedroom just before we children were put to bed; this not only provided a light for us to undress but was supposed to take off the chill of the room, although I was convinced it made very little difference! For many centuries, and even when I lived in High Pennard during the 1950's and 60's, during the summer months, all the local people got up at five in the morning, and were in bed by nine o'clock at night, thus making use of every hour of daylight.

The surrounding cottages and farms were all built in a similar lay-out. Cliff Cottage, when I knew it, had remained the same for well over a hundred years. It also had a typical Gower farmhouse porch. The only slight difference was the position of the staircase. This was tucked away in the corner of the main living room, right alongside the 'inglenook' seat at the side of the huge open grate. It even had its own small, latched wooden door, opening onto a steep, narrow, winding timber stairway, which turned over the chimney to the floor above. Halfway up this stair-case was a niche cut into the wall where a candle or oil-lamp could be placed in a strategic position to light the way to bed.

Almost every cottage had its pig-sty, which was usually at the bottom of the garden. Beaufort had quite an elaborate affair, with room for at least three pigs. Cliff Cottage also had quite a large pig sty, positioned right at the edge of the cliff. Pigs were comparatively cheap animals to keep, and certainly helped to make any family's diet far more interesting, as well as being very nutritious. In Winter, when they were kept in, they were fed on mangels, which could be grown on any spare piece of ground. Then in Summer they would be allowed to roam, and brought in at night. They would eat literally anything. The Beaufort pigs in wartime were fed with any scraps of food left over from the inn, together with the odd small potatoes, and I have even seen Aunty 'Ru' give them limpets which she had gathered from the rocks. On other occasions they would just be thrown the washing-up water containing all the peelings and scraps, but hopefully no soap!

The other small building at the bottom of every garden was, of course, the 'tŷ-bach' (privy). Every cottage had its own earth closet, which in early years was a trench dug into the ground, over which was placed a rough seat with the requisite hole. Later some sort of container which could be emptied when necessary, was placed under the hole. Beaufort had two such closets, which served the busy, often crowded inn, right up to the day it ceased to be a pub in 1939!

Work

From 1800 the men would be working in the quarry; and in the early days indulge perhaps in a spot of smuggling; some, like John Timothy, might even work with the Oyster boats in Mumbles, but for all the families, even those living in the inns, the main occupation which went on throughout the year was farming. They were constantly pitting their wits and muscles against a difficult and unpredictable climate, in order to supply themselves with food and possibly have some over to use for 'bartering'.

Many of the Cottagers in High Pennard would make arrangements with the larger farms, such as Great Kittle Farm (120 acres); Hunts (100 acres); Hael (60 acres); and Widegate (30 acres), that in return for having a row of potatoes in one of their fields, the whole family would turn out and help plant all the farmers' potatoes and later help to lift them. Instead of wages, some labourers would take home eggs, milk or even a piece of pig, that had been salted down. In his diary John Timothy reports how he "Went home about potatoes" on Tuesday, 29th March, 1864, and the very next day, "Went to Pwldye again about the 'tatoes'"– obviously the harvesting of potatoes was an important event in the yearly calender. Very few things needed to be actually 'bought'. Even John Timothy, living on his own in lodgings in Mumbles, only had to buy a few basics. Here is one of his grocery bills in 1864:

Grocers Had With John Bevan in 1864

Tea & sugar (5 separate entries)	1 .. 11
Meat	1 .. 00
pills and watch key	1 .. 7
1 pound butter	1 .. 1
herings	3
Butter	1 .. 3
tea sugar Butter	3 .. 2
oil	2

Farming at this time was very basic. The only saleable things from 1800-1900 were wheat, barley (for brewing), beef, mutton, a few eggs, poultry and a bacon pig or so. The only fertilisers were farm yard humus, and, of course, lime. Some of the fields were used to grow potatoes, a few cabbages and some swedes. Other fields were sown with wheat, the husks were taken to be ground into flour and brought back to the farm ready for the bread baking. People just lived off the land. They might sell a bullock or two. We know that from the earliest times, John Jenkins fished and caught lobsters and crabs. These would no doubt have been used to barter for other goods from the farms and cottages in the area, as well as supplementing the diet of his own large family. At the height of the limestone industry, Pyle Corner was known as Marchant's Cross. This cross roads leading to Pwlldu Bay, was where local farmers from Pwlldu, High Pennard and Bishopston would bring their goods to sell to the sailors and quarrymen.

The larger farms employed many farm hands and most of the men from the High Pennard cottages are referred to as 'agricultural labourers' in the Census Returns from 1831-1891.

These labourers would be expected to mow an acre of hay by hand with a scythe. This would take them most of the day, and they were paid 2/6. Hoeing swedes was sometimes done by children and women; again pay was paltry, something like 1d for 40 yards

The men who were listed as actually living at the farmhouses, were unmarried labourers. In the 1851 Census, there were five such men living in 'Hunts' Farm. These men received about £5 a year, which was paid at Christmas. In 1871, when the well-known Beynon family from Rhossilli took over the farm, they were farming 130 acres, and by 1881 this had become 200 acres.

The Parish Marriage Records also reveal that these larger farming families, many of whom had farmed the same land for well over a hundred years, made every effort, not only to keep their estates in the family, but also to arrange for their daughters to make as advantageous a marriage as possible. A perfect illustration of this was in the early 1840's, when brother and sister, William and Catherine Jones of Widegate farm, respectively married two people of Highway; of course this was not to be wondered at, when one realises that both farms are only separated by 'Smugglers Lane'! Catherine's husband, Richard Griffiths, was the son of John Griffiths, who had been Arthur's right-hand man, at the height of the smuggling days 50 years earlier.

Even in this small, self contained, community, there would seem to be very loosely defined social strata. The marriages seemed to be 'arranged' or at least 'approved', and most couples were in their early 20's before marrying. From the weddings 'in the valley' it is noticeable that most of the children married into families which farmed some land; such as the Davies' family of High Pennard; the Jones of Hareslade; and Samuel Jones who married a daughter from Great Kittle. Craftsmen were also considered as on this level of society; William Jones of 'Beaufort' had married Elizabeth Jones of Widegate, whose father was a weaver. The 'crofters' of High Pennard, who were agricultural labourers and labourers in the quarry, tended to marry people from a neighbouring cottage who were similarly employed. In 1871, Will Bevan, son of labourer David Bevan, who lived in a cottage in High Pennard, married Elizabeth Phillips who lived near him, and whose father, Samuel was also an agricultural labourer. It is also significant that none of these people could sign their names; while by the same date all the men from both inns in Pwlldu could write a very reasonable signature.

The Census Returns also reveal that in a household, a sharp distinction was drawn between an agricultural labourer and a farmer's son, even if they are the same age.

Education

The Parish Marriage registers give further insight into the standard of education during this period. Although many of the men could sign their names on their wedding certificates, they would not necessarily have been really literate. Before 1880, very few girls could write anything but an 'X' on their certificates. There is little surprise in this finding, as Vancouver states in 1808:

> *". . . the peasant's mind should never be inspired with a desire to amend his circumstances by the quitting of his caste; but every means the most benevolent and feeling heart can devise should be employed to make that situation as comfortable and as happy to him as possible."*

In other words, the best way of 'educating' the labouring population of Pwlldu and the neighbouring farms was to foster in them a pride in doing a job well; this would include the quarrying and loading of limestone; their many farming tasks; not to mention the making up and repairing of the only road to Bishopston, and ultimately Swansea!

During the eighteenth century there was very little provision for education. At the beginning of the century there is a report that a certain *"Catherine Rees of the parish of Bishopston, did by will, dated 3rd Sept, 1728, give the sum of £100 for ever . . .*

that the yearly profits thereof should be applied towards the education of six poor children as had a legal settlement in the parish . . ."

So certainly no Pwlldu or High Pennard child could be one of these 'lucky few' as none of them lived in the Parish of Bishopston. Neither were they likely to be one of the ten children who were taught at Murton, by a widow of 56, in a small room in her cottage.

It is interesting that most of the young children in the two Pwlldu inns, and indeed in the rest of the area, between the ages of 6 and 11, are described as 'scholars' in the Census returns from 1851-1891. Yet it is highly unlikely that any of these children attended any sort of school before 1870, when school attendance became compulsory. The young children from High Pennard and Pwlldu would have had to walk up the long valley, or probably taken the shorter but still tortuous route down the cliff on the Pennard side, through Pwldye woods, past Knapp farm, over the fields and down to Bishopston School, which at this time was situated below the church, at the head of Bishopston Valley. Later, young Eddie Butcher and his two sisters were to take this same route to the same school, and he has described what a difficult and long route it was for a young child.

In 1847, an Assistant Commissioner reported on a school at Bishopston. This consisted of a large roofed area abutting the church wall. Here the church catechism was taught. The children sat on crude wooden benches, their only 'desk' being two planks nailed on poles driven into the floor. In 1850, the building became a Church school and was taken over by the National Society for Promoting the Education of the Poor in the Principles of the Established Church. The Commissioner remarked how most of the children were drawn from *"the labouring population who were employed either in agriculture or oyster catching."*

We know that it was common practice for the older children to be kept home at Springtime to plant crops. For similar reasons, there was a severe drop in attendance during the Summer months, when the harvesting of crops took place. Of course if older pupils stayed away, there would be no-one to accompany the little ones to school, which was particularly necessary for the children of Pwlldu and High Pennard, who had difficult journeys to make. An examination of the old school log books reveals that the school often had to close when there was a severe outbreak of an infectious disease. This occurred in 1880, when there was an outbreak of scarlet fever, and again in 1885, when the school had to close for two weeks, owing to an epidemic of typhoid fever. Even as late as 1936 an outbreak of diphtheria closed the school for a short time. These severe outbreaks of infectious diseases help to explain the many infant and child deaths we have found recorded in the parish records, pertaining to the families in Pwlldu and High Pennard. Even when the children did get to school, both sexes were not always treated alike; one of the older women from Pwlldu who attended Bishopston school at the turn of the century stated that:

> *". . . although we had quite a good teacher, the girls were never given the chance the boys had. Often we had to stay at home and help with the family. Even when we did go, we often didn't have the same lessons as the boys did. The boys did more mathematics and reading than we did."*

In 1893 the leaving age was officially 11 years, and in 1899, this became 12 years of age.

From the Parish Records and the Census Returns, we learn that it was common for girls of 12 to be fully employed as an 'indoor servant' or 'female servant', and even in one case, young Ann Phillip, aged 12, is described as a nurse, probably to look after the four younger children of the family, including a baby of six months. Young Selina Webborn, also aged 12, whose grand-father was head of the household, and employed as an Oyster-Dredger, was expected to act as a laundress for the whole family! Even as late as 1914, Molly James describes how a very young girl of 12 or 13 years of age was employed as a house maid in Beaufort.

There was an apprentice system for the boys, and certainly many did have a chance to learn a trade, such as weaving, or to become a wheelwright, blacksmith or even a maltster! But again these apprenticeships tended to be kept in the family, and skills were traditionally passed down through the generations. We have already observed this happening in the limestone industry where even skills such as lime-burning, or becoming lime captains, tended to remain in the same family. Like the girls, many twelve year old boys were employed as a 'servant' in the better off families, or in the larger farms; some were even from large farming families themselves, yet it was probably thought to be to their advantage to learn a trade away from home. One such example in this area, is found in the census return for 1871. The Davies family were farming 25 acres in High Pennard. Here we find young William Tucker, aged 12, being employed as a servant. His birth place is given as Penmaen and he is probably from the well-known farming family of the Tuckers of Penmaen; the same family as Elizabeth Tucker came from when she married John Jenkin in 1803. It is not unusual to find young grandsons of 12 or 14 'working on the farm' of their grand-parents. The Davies family, farming 30 acres in Bishopston, employed two young grandsons on their farm, both of whom had been born in London. The two elderly Gwynn farmers in High Pennard employed a young boy of 14 as a House-Servant to look after them. These young girls and boys could only hope to climb even one step of the social ladder by making advantageous marriages. Yet if someone was as determined and enterprising as John Timothy, there would seem to be some opportunity for further study, even after one had left school for many years. His hard backed exercise book, with its exquisitely decorated title page, is proof of an education that was quite exceptional for one of the labouring class in the early 19th century.

The handwriting throughout the book is not only clear and neat, but shows a very real pride in his work. The headings are attractively set out in bold decorative script, and when writing out 'problems' in Arithmetic, the initial letters are beautifully decorated. The arithmetic rules are quite advanced and cover compound addition, subtraction and multiplication; vulgar and decimal fractions; the reduction of decimals; and

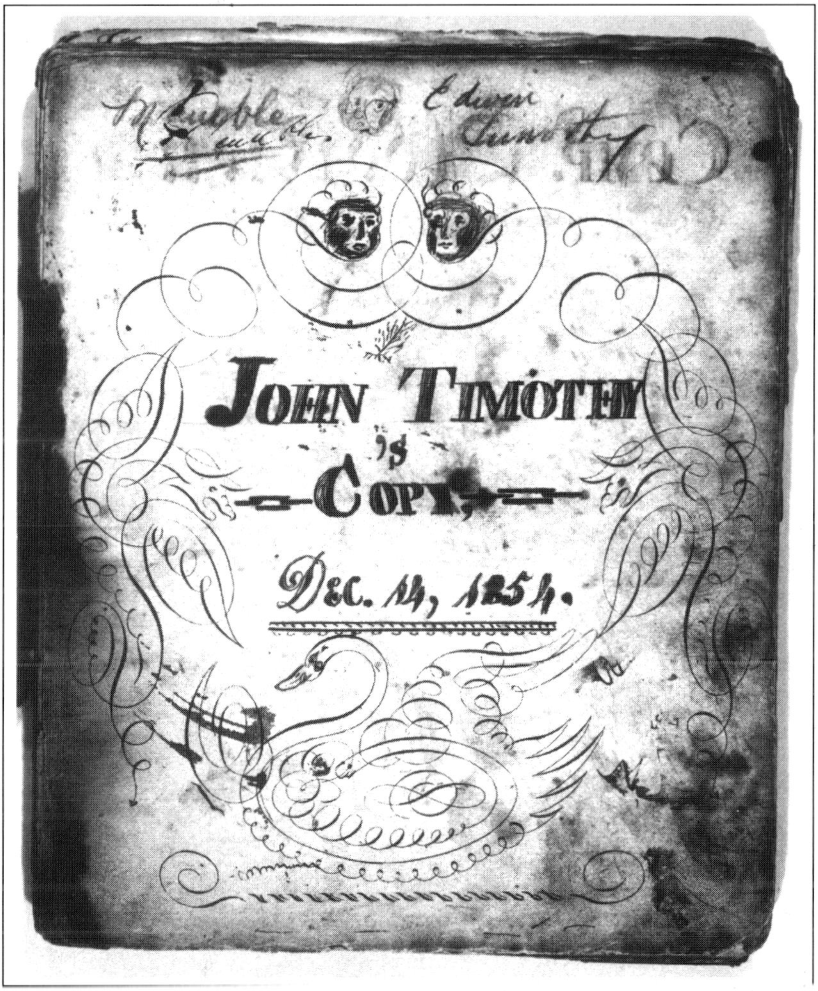

The cover of John Timothy's Notebook, 1854.

mensuration. Today's schooboys, with their micro-chips, pocket calculators and personal computers, might blanch at the rows and rows of neatly handwritten figures. These rules are then applied to the practical work that was obviously common practice at the time: Joiners' Work, Carpenters' Work, Of Walling, Of Gable Ends, Of Paving and Plasterers' Work. The notebook states that: *"John Timothy wrote this on February 1st,*

1862 – Being One Schooldays Night and Very dark But not Much Wind But raining smale rain." He was aged about 22.

WORK AND PLAY

Women's Work is Never Done!

Women's work was hard and often had to be carried out either just after a birth or when a woman was heavily pregnant. Most families were large and when babies died, others were quickly in their place, and would often take the name of the dead baby. Apart from household chores, women would be expected to help out in the fields during harvest, potato planting, or any other busy time. We know that some worked helping to load the limestone into the boats. Many farmers' wives would have to do the milking of ewes and then use that milk, curdled with vinegar, to make cheese. Baking was a daily chore. This was in the bee-hive ovens that most cottagers possessed. The interior of these ovens was made of fire-bricks. and they could take nine or ten loaves at a time. Even as late as the 1940's, 'Ma' Jenkins used her bee-hive oven, swearing that no oven, even her new, black iron range, could bake bread in quite the same way. In the early days, and right up to the first World War, white bread was only provided on Sundays. 'Everyday' bread had the bran left in and provided a very coarse textured loaf. Flat bakestone loaves, about one inch thick, were made from barley. Such a loaf was always collected by young Eddie Butcher on his way home from school.

Many times, as a child I had watched Ma Jenkins use her bee-hive oven. The best fuel for these ovens was without doubt 'smitty sticks'. These were placed in the base of the oven and set alight. In a fairly short time the bricks would become very hot. The next step was for the embers to be scraped out and the loaves put in. The door was then sealed with the white or red clay easily found in Pwlldu Bay. After two hours the baking was complete. The oven was then re-fuelled with more 'smitty sticks' ready for the next burning. Of course, sometimes wood from the beach was used, as smitty sticks were not always available, but I was assured that the best baking was always from the smitty sticks, which produced a far greater heat than normal drift-wood.

Many wives brewed beer for their own households. Nettle wine was also a great favourite . Both inns, and several of the farms in High Pennard, regularly produced their own and it was particularly popular during potato planting and picking time, and also at harvest. In these early times it was often served in the huge red pottery 'cloams' which had been brought over from Devon by the 'muffies'. These were particularly useful for carrying out beer to the workers in the fields.

Most women, especially in isolated areas such as Pwlldu and High Pennard, acted as unpaid doctors and mid-wives. Remedies for all kinds of illnesses were handed down through the generations. Elderberry wine was a 'Jenkins special,' and if I ever showed sign of a cold or cough then I was dosed with 'Ma Jenkins's home made elderberry wine. This continued to be a 'Jenkins Special' and was produced by Ma Jenkins throughout her life. Alf Jenkins, who was known to love his 'pop', always carried a bottle in his waistcoat pocket. David Jenkins suffered very badly with rheumatism, particularly in his later years, and Alf insisted that the best remedy his grandfather could find was dried broom or sorrel made into a kind of tea.

Play

We only have to look at John Timothy's Diary, to realise that walking long distances was quite normal. Indeed, Pwlldu people, down the years, were all good walkers – they had to be if they wanted to get out of the bay! This applied to women as well as men. Before 1900 when they had the time, they would walk into Bishopston, sometimes listening out for the pack horses to take them into Swansea Market, but more often they would walk across the Common, down Bishopston Road, where at the bottom of the hill the Mumbles train would take them into town. The return journey would be the same way, a train to Bishopston Road (now Blackpill), a walk over the common to Murton, and then across the fields, through Pwll-dye Woods, down the track to the bay; and, of course, those who were living in High Pennard would have another steep climb up the cliff the other side.

Life was not all work. The bars at the various Inns, both on the beach and higher up at the top of the valley, were well patronised by most labourers and farmers, some would say too well patronised! People were spoilt for choice. Many people brewed their own beer for family and friends, some even sold it on a small scale. But for a good night out the men went to one of the many 'pubs' in the area. In this early period, Ship and Beaufort did good business. In Murton, The Plough and Harrow, which had been in the village since 1583, when it was an old coaching inn, was a much favoured drinking venue. The Cross Inn (now named The Bishopston Valley Hotel), situated in the middle of the village, was another favourite. Opposite, was the Joiners' Arms which had developed from a carpenters workshop, and had become an inn by about 1850. There was also an inn called The New Inn, overlooking Bishopston Valley. There is a large cellar in the house, where smugglers were said to have hidden 'the goodies' carried up the Bishopston Valley from the French luggers that had brought the contraband into Pwlldu Bay. All these public houses are mentioned by John Timothy in his diary, together with 'Collinses' (later known as The Beaufort Arms), situated at the top of Kittle Hill. John Timothy's bill for:

> *'Beer Drunk in John Rogers'* is a much bigger bill than his grocery account for a similar period:

8 entries (settled)	14-11-10	
Credit	10- 8- 0	
	4- 3-10	
	1-10- 0	5-13-0

The £10-8-0 credit, could well have been in lieu of some bartering of oysters, or even fresh vegetables from his small-holding. Barely a day is recorded when he did not imbibe a minimum of three or four pints of beer, especially on a Sunday, between church services! An example of a not untypical day is the entry for Saturday 13th of March, 1864:

> *"Went to the Swansea Arms with George Jenkins of Heale. Met Wm Gwyn, Thomas John and William Davies, Southgate. Went from there to the Joiners Arms with Wm Gwyn. Came down by the 7 o'clock train to Bishopston Road. Wm Gwyn, Wm Webborn and myself walked over the common to Murton. Went into the Plough & Harrow. Drank a glass or two of beer then went west."*

Four pubs in one day, and no doubt several pints of beer! Little wonder he *"Sleeped home all night."*

Another entry from a diary of the same period, shows that not all drinking had pleasant consequences. The diary of J. G. Hancorne, the well-known agricultural surveyor and auctioneer of Kittle Hill Farm, reports how on 27th Aug, 1840 –

> *". . . ride to Pooldye to receive Roper's rent and drank three pints of his ale which has made me very ill all this day."*

This was more than likely Roper's own home-brew..

The pubs were not just there for drinking, but were centres of all kinds of social activity. Alf Jenkins of Ship played the accordion and the fiddle; he in turn had been taught by his father and grandfather. Apparently many musical evenings had been spent in the bars of Beaufort and Ship. Another entry in John Timothy's diary records how on a visit to the Beaufort Arms at Kittle:

> *"The music men came in then or a little before 12. Four brass instruments and a drum . . ."*

and on Thursday 18th February 1864, he spent an evening at Murton Club and obviously joined in the music-making, as he:

". . . stayed there a little Wile had my concertina brought it With me to Mumbles."

Apparently dancing often took place, and the Gower form of 'stepping' was very popular in bars. This would have been performed by men; women who wanted to dance would have to wait for the 'cutting of the wheat', when the evening before reaping was to begin, many barns were used for the harvest supper and folk dancing afterwards.

The men also had their draughts and quoits clubs. Card games were very popular and, since early times, the Malt House in Pwlldu saw many games going on all night, often accompanied by heavy betting. We already know that the Malt House itself was acquired in this way, and the 'Jones' brothers told me that they had won two fields from the 'Hunts' boys in a game of cards that had taken place at the same venue! These water meadows that bordered the stream in the bay itself were farmed by them for many years and were sometimes referred to in the Jones family as 'Hunts Fields'!

Church and Chapel

There was no hard and fast division between Church and Chapel; many people went to both, and members of a family might be mixed, some calling themselves church, some chapel. The people of Pwlldu, High Pennard and the surrounding farms had a good choice of places of worship.

The origin of St Mary's Pennard, is still not clear, but it seems possible that an early Celtic Church cell was present within the boundary of the Norman parish. What is particularly interesting is that one of these possible sites could even have been on Pwll Du Head itself; this is based on the evidence of an old field name. The present church was certainly there during the eighteenth and nineteenth centuries. In 1838, when the advowson of the church passed to Major Penrice, the church building was restored. This was the church of the Parish of Pennard and as such recorded all the deaths, baptisms and weddings in the Parish. Pwlldu and High Pennard are in the Parish and it is likely that many of the families whose history we have been considering attended services at Pennard and were certainly buried in the churchyard. From High Pennard they would have followed the 'funeral route' behind Webb's Cottage, over the fields to Widegates, and then up the track which comes out immediately opposite the church. Pwlldu folk would take the same route but mourners would have the additional climb up the cliff.

In Bishopston, the church of St. Teilo, occupies one of the earliest sites of Christian settlements in Wales. Its long history probably dates back to about A.D. 1130. Its present fabric is either late 12th century or early 13th century. It was also restored by Thomas Penrice of Kilvrough in 1851, and the date of its restoration is recorded above the porch. Situated right at the head of the Bishopston Valley, it also provided a place of worship for both High Pennard and Pwlldu folks, particularly as many of the families were originally from this Parish and still had many family members living in Bishopston. High Pennard worshippers would have taken the same route as the children did to get to school; that is down the cliff, up through the Pwldye Woods to Knap, and then over the fields, dropping down to the church.

In Bishopston itself, or to be more accurate between Bishopston and Murton, situated in the fields, was Providence Chapel. This was one of the oldest non-conformist chapels in Gower and was probably built in 1807. Its foundation was due to the efforts of the Reverend David Davies, and some of the first meetings were held in High Pennard House (later known as Cliff Cottage). This could well be the service that John Timothy says he went to on Sunday 21st February, 1864:

> *"I went to Highpenard to Mary's to hear Mr Williams preach a Sermond at 2-."*

The next month, on March 20th, he describes how he:

> *"Went home, had dinner went to Highpenard Church and heard him preach again on 7 chapter and 25 verse of hebrews."*

The preacher is the same Mr Williams who had preached the previous month, so it is safe to assume that the service was in the same cottage. In the 1851 Religious Census it is stated that in Bishopston Church there was an average morning congregation of 30, with 40 in the afternoon. Some of these would no doubt be regular worshippers, but others would be like John Timothy, who liked nothing more than visiting as many churches or chapels on a Sunday, and enjoying as many sermons as he could cram into a day! Such a Sunday is described by him in his entry for Sunday, 28th February, 1864.

This is a particularly interesting entry as we are able to identify many of his companions. 'J. Jones' would have been Jane Jones of 'Beaufort'. Mary was very probably 'Mary Davies' who was soon to become his wife. Rachel was John's sister. The party split up, half of them visiting the Chapel, while Jane Jones and John Timothy went to Pennard Church. After the service ended, they walked over 'the Cwmbs' to Parkmill, where again the party split up. William Gwyn stayed at the Chapel in Parkmill, while the rest of his companions walked on up the steep hill to Penmaen Church. Obviously, distance was no problem for John Timothy or his friends from High Pennard and Bishopston, who frequently joined him on his Sunday excursions. There were well used footpaths to all the places he mentions, and indeed these same paths were used just as much, well into the 1950's and most of them can be walked today. One such Sunday walk is vividly illustrated by another entry in the Diary, dated Sunday 31st, January, 1864, when he was lodging in Mumbles.

> *"Rose at 9 o'clock, had breakfast, put on my clothes and then started for Pwldye. Got there at 1 o'clock. The weather fine, then it rained in the morning. Very smart wind. Stayed in the house until 5 then went to Knap with Wm Lloyd, John Morgan and Wm and myself went to Bishopston together. Met with Philip Beynon of Bishopston, went to Kittle together. We drank 1 pint in 'Collinses'. Started for Parkmill. Got down to the Chapel, met them coming from Penmaen Church. Came back and got to Mumbles at quarter to 1."*

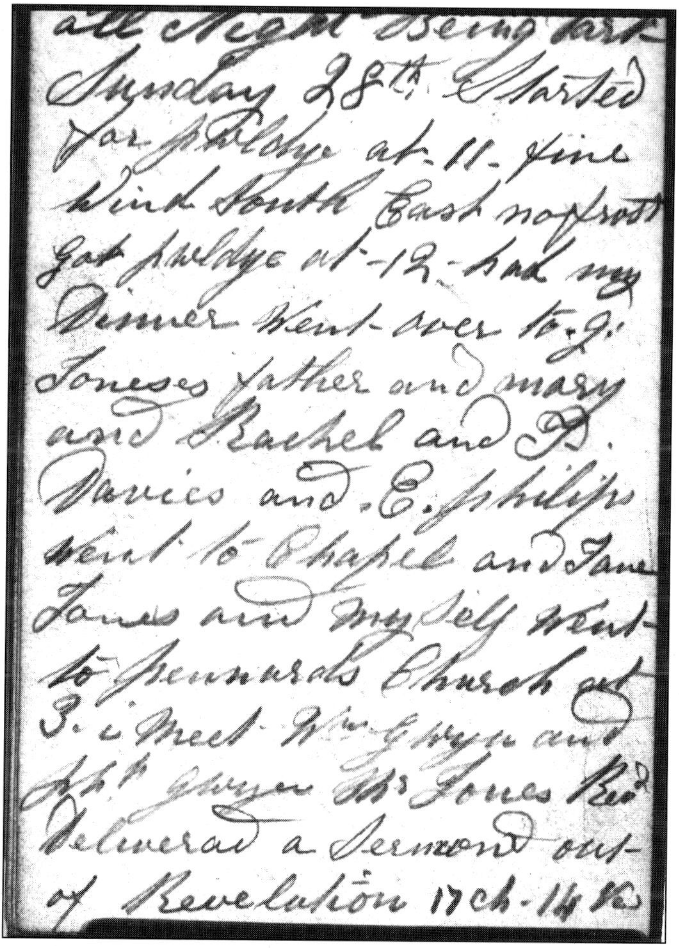
all Night Being dark
Sunday 28th Started
for Pwlldye at 11 fine
Wind South East no frost
Got Pwlldye at 12 had my
Dinner Went over to J.
Joneses Father and Mary
and Rachel and D.
Davies and E. Philips
Went to Chapel and Jane
Jones and my Self Went
to Pennards Church at
3. i Meet Wm Glyn and
Jn Glyn Mr Jones Revd
Delivered a Sermond out
of Revelation 17ch 14 Ve

Page of John Timothy's Diary, Sunday 28th Feb. 1864.

The William Lloyd mentioned, was the village carpenter, wheelwright and blacksmith. His workshops were situated behind the public house, The Joiners' Arms. He was a great friend of John Timothy, and often accompanied him on a Sunday excursion, when he would be free of his work at the Joiners.

No mention of a horse – all this was done on foot. From Mumbles John Timothy would probably have climbed the steep path up to the top of Oystermouth village and gone through the lanes to Murton, on through Bishopston, over the fields, past Knap, through the woods to his father's cottage at Pwldye. An afternoon at home, then he retraced his steps, this time taking the steep and very twisting path behind the church, up to the top of Kittle Hill. After a quick pint at 'Collinses' (The Beaufort Arms), on over the fields, and finally dropping down to Parkmill. The most amazing end to this day is that he walked back to Mumbles, probably going from Parkmill over the Common, arriving home at 1 a.m. in the morning – no doubt ready to wake bright and early for work on the following day!

This then is a glimpse at the social life of the community of Pwlldu and its immediate environs, in the years before 1900; and of course many aspects of the life were to continue well into the next century. A closely knit community, that supplied special skills, seasonal labour, and rudimentary education. The hub of their lives was Sunday services in church or chapel, weddings and funerals, visits to the pubs, occasional fairs and other revels; these are what drew the community together. Courtesy, good will and endurance were also an inherent part of their day to day living. These were people who were rooted deep in a hundred years of pastoral life, in a landscape of unsurpassed beauty; high cliffs, gentle valley and dancing river, a sea that had not only provided them with a living, but could change its mood overnight; enchanting in fair weather, but in a hard winter, full of peril for man and beast. Although thinly populated the whole area was a neighbourhood; people were ready to help each other, knowing that they might at any time need serious help themselves. They shared enjoyment of the fixed high days and holidays, and drew steadiness from the work needed, year in, year out, to win food and livelihood from the soil.

Continuity and Change

The first two decades of the present century are a time not yet quite out of mind. The grandchildren that I talked to, now in their eighties or nineties, had long and uncluttered memories, and could recall scraps of their own experience, or repeat what they had heard from their elders, with every detail vivid and correct. What is more, they were country people, who took their time in telling their tales, trying to pass on the flavour of life as it had been. All their stories are steeped in a sense of character and time. This is the nearer view that forms the second part of my book. It almost wrote itself, as I sifted through the tapes of the many conversations that I had had with men and women born and brought up in Pwlldu and its immediate vicinity.

One such person was Mrs Margaret Snell, who now lives in Pwlldu Lane. Her grandmother, Mrs Matilda Morgan, in 1906, was left a widow at the young age of 32. Her husband had been the Manager of Lloyds Bank in Wind Street. Deeply shocked and with seven young children to bring up, she decided that one of the best things she could do was to rent a holiday cottage in High Pennard. No doubt the complete change of scene and indeed living conditions would provide the challenge she needed to come to terms with her grief. Her children obviously loved Pwlldu and like so many children before and since, considered the bay their own personal place and resented anyone else visiting it. They continued to rent the cottage until 1912. Mrs Snell gave me some fascinating details about the kind of life they lived during their holidays.

The girls, after visiting Bishopston for church or chapel would often have to find their way back to High Pennard in the dark. The long walk down Pwlldu Lane, then the steep cliff path down past Rachel's Cottage, over the bridge, and then the long climb up to the other side, was undertaken, with only the light of a candle stuck in a jam-jar to light their way. Although there was a bee-hive oven in the cottage, Mrs Morgan did not want to do too much baking on holiday, so the children were sent for bread from a bakery situated at the top of the Valley, somewhere near the old school. The family owned a donkey which was often used to carry loads up and down the steep cliffs. The bread would be securely tied into two clean white pillowcases which were then slung over the donkey's back and the bread safely carried home.

Two very tragic accidents occurred while they were in High Pennard. One afternoon as the two older brothers were in the garden of the cottage they suddenly heard some faint but frantic calls for help. The stillness of the Valley together with the lack of trees would probably have aided the sound to travel. Both boys tore down the cliff and quickly located the cries coming from some people standing on the edge of the deep pool that forms on the bend of the river. They learned that a small boy had fallen in and could no longer be seen. Taking turns, the two boys dived into the cold but clear water and eventually located the small body. Sadly their efforts were in vain as the boy was already dead. The other accident took place near the small shop that was located opposite the school and used by the children to buy sweets. There had been many storms in the Valley and the river was swollen and running very fast. One small lad lost his cap in the water and in trying to retrieve it, lost his balance and fell into the river. Before he could be rescued he was swept away and drowned.

Some of the Morgan children were very musical and wanted a piano at the cottage so that they could continue practising during the holidays. A piano was duly bought and a horse drawn cart procured to bring it down the cliff on the Bishopston side of the Valley. The path on the other side of the cliff was quite impossible for such a heavy load, so the three brothers actually carried it between them all the way up to the cottage at the top of the cliff.

This steep, rutted track that leads to Pwlldu from High Pennard is remembered by Mr Arthur Jones, who described it as:

Photograph of painting by W. Whitby, 1888.
Note steep but smoother road to High Pennard, also garage outside Beaufort gate.

> *". . . lovely – steep yes – but much smoother than it is today. It had to be, you see, it was the main road to Swansea, and more importantly Swansea Market. The crofters of High Pennard had to keep it in good condition – their livelihood depended on it."*

The three 'Johnnies' were the men mainly responsible for keeping the road in a reasonable condition: Johnny Phillips of Cliff Cottage, Johnny Webb and Johnny Pritchard. Using 'sledgies' (sledge hammers) with long handles of hazel wood, in order to resist vibration, they would break up the larger projecting ridges of stone, and then carry up the path small heaps of egg-shaped stones, which would be used to fill in any gaps and try to smooth the surface. This was often a long and tedious task, not to mention the hazard of the white dust from the broken limestone, which not only covered the immediate undergrowth but presented quite a hazard to the men.

The road on the East side of the bay was similarly maintained, and was a lot smoother than today's rough track, and could be used by simple horse drawn carts and traps.

Each Johnny owned a 'Slide Car'. These wooden sledges had been in use for many years where the roads were too steep or rough for a wheeled vehicle. In early years its forerunner had been the truckle cart, which was a form of wooden sledge on wheels, with a high frame behind the horse; this vehicle was still in use on many Gower farms until the 1890's. Today a smaller version of the sledge is used in Clovelly, North Devon, to carry produce up and down the main, very steep cobbled road that leads to the harbour. In High Pennard, every Saturday, throughout the year, farm produce such as rabbits, poultry, butter, cream, cheese and any vegetables in season, were loaded onto the horse drawn slide cars and taken down the cliff path as far as the Beaufort gates. Here there was a small building known as the cart shed or garage. Inside were stored three wheeled traps. The horses would be harnessed into the traps; the goods carefully transferred from the slide cars, which would then be parked on the grass verge bordering the river.

The crofters would set out for market at about 8 a.m. and would not return until after 2 p.m. The men were usually accompanied by their wives, who often off-loaded their goods to regular clients in the market, or sometimes sold the produce themselves. Apparently, it was quite common for the men to visit a few pubs in Swansea, before picking up the women for the journey home.

On reaching Pwlldu, it was the women again who unloaded their weekly market purchases, transferred them to the slide cars, reharnessed the horses, and got ready for the steep climb back up the cliff. The horses, as soon as they were given the signal would start off at a brisk rate, their hooves sending up a shower of sparks as they tried to gain a purchase on the stones. The opening burst of speed was essential to tackle the steepness of the cliff path, but it could not be sustained, and after just ten yards or more, they had to stop for a rest. Thus they made their way to the top of the cliff and without any difficulty would find the way to their respective crofts. Only if the loads were particularly heavy or needed attention, were they led; usually the women would follow on behind and make their own way up the cliff.

This was a hard time for the wives and daughters of both the farmers and labourers. It was they who held everything together; and a wife with a large family of children to be clothed and fed would be given little if any housekeeping money. We know that the High Pennard wives from the small farms earned some money from marketing some of their produce, but often they would have to find other ways to supplement this small income. Arthur and Harry Phillips recall how their grandmother, Mary Phillips, could turn her hand to anything and often went out to do painting and decorating. In Summer she walked to Swansea with baskets of gooseberries picked from the many bushes that grew in Cliff Cottage garden (that were still there when I was a girl). All water for drinking had to be carried from wells or springs, the one used by the High Pennard crofters was situated right out on the cliffs below Body Acre Cottage. Older children looked after younger ones, and all had their tasks around the house and farm. They would have to help feed chickens and geese and shut them up at night, and gather in the eggs, making sure they traced any hen who had 'stolen her nest'. Most of the women had a far lonelier life than their menfolk; although they did manage to go to market together once a week, that was all the time they could spare. The men used to buy and sell stock at distant farms or visit horse fairs, and as we know many of them drank far too much, there and in their local pub, the Beaufort.

One such time would be after their trip to Swansea. While their wives would be toiling up the cliff, they would normally go into the pub 'for a quick one', which of course it rarely was!! Indeed Johnny Phillips often found the journey up the steep cliff difficult, so his wife, after unloading the slide car at Cliff Cottage, would send the horse and vehicle back down the path, to wait at the gates of Beaufort, in order to carry the master back home when he finally appeared.

John and Mary Phillips outside their cottage in High Pennard.

On one such occasion the slide car duly arrived back at Cliff Cottage without its usual occupant! Mary Phillips, alarmed at her husband's absence, went down to Beaufort to see what had happened. A search party was set up, and at first had no success in finding the reveller, who had obviously fallen from the slide car on its journey up the cliff. Then Johnny Webb had a brilliant idea – they would set the furze on either side of the path alight! As the flames progressed, the muffled cries of Johnny Phillips could be heard and he was quickly located.

Johnny Phillips and his wife Mary lived with their four children in Cliff Cottage at the turn of the century. It is reputed that Johnny even had his own private path to Beaufort, known by older residents as 'Johnny's Path'. Right in front of the cottage is a high projecting piece of cliff. Johnny would make for this, and as soon as possible he would drop down behind the rocks, immediately being out of the view of his wife Mary. He could then make his way undetected, to the Beaufort, where he could meet his mates for their usual convivial evening.

Johnny Phillips' eldest surviving grandson, Mr Harry Phillips, knew his grandparents well and often visited them in High Pennard. He confirmed that drinking sessions at the Beaufort were a regular part of Pwlldu life. Henry Jones of Hunts Farm, who was a butcher and a farmer, often joined his friends from High Pennard, but was very rarely drunk. I was told that this was not because of any high moral principles, but because he hated to spend money!! Often on a late dark night, he would find himself accompanying two or three very unsteady crofters, back up the steep, stony path to the cliff top. He would not have gone far when he heard a voice calling out to him, *"Henry, Henry, wait a minute, come down here, I'm in the bushes."*

Once the inebriated men had fallen into the furze that grew thickly either side of the path, they found it almost impossible to get up without assistance. Henry Jones would have to retrace his steps, locate the slurred voice, and then with a great deal of pulling and heaving, the unsteady man would be hauled upright and set on his way. The onerous task was not complete, the worst part was yet to come! Somehow they would have to be supported and brought up the rough very steep path to the top of the cliff at High Pennard. As Harry said, *"Once they were on the top, it was alright"*. Mr Eddie Butcher, whose father was the landlord at Beaufort at this time, has told how some mornings, he would come across many a recumbent figure in the furze who had failed to make it home the night before.

Drunken men were not the only heavy loads that the slide cars carried; they were used to transport any heavy articles that needed to be moved from one side of the cliff to the other. One of Arthur Jones' proudest memories was the occasion when as a fifteen year old, he was asked by his father to help John Webb bring a heavy farm implement across the valley to Bishopston, where there was to be a sale the following day. Arthur, with great enjoyment recalled the incident:

"Arthur, how are you going to get it over to the other side?"
"Oh, I don't know, it could be difficult," I replied.
"Borrow my slide car" said my father ,"then after you've delivered the implement to the sale you can bring it back here."
So, I hitched up our horse to the slide-car and led him over the fields, down the cliff, then up the other side , all the way to Webb's. There I loaded up the cart, and went back the same way. It wasn't easy because the road was still very steep and stony, but I managed it. You see the old horse was used to it. When I got back to the farm my father praised me. It was the first time I'd done such a difficult job all on my own. I was thrilled"

Sheep Washing and Shearing

In early Summer, the sound of outraged bleating would echo across the Valley; this was the signal that the time honoured practice of sheep washing was about to take place. A deep pool alongside the river, on the bend where the water is at its deepest, would have been specially hollowed out by the farmers. Sheep washing was one of the most important events in the farming year and the whole operation needed quite a few men to carry it out. There was never any shortage of volunteers; it was quite usual for any able bodied men in the community to help out the farmers on such occasions – but besides this, it was great fun! Even regular summer visitors used to help out. One such man was George Tongrove, from Morriston, who had a summer bungalow at Pyle, and loved nothing better than helping out the farming community in any way he could. The well known Barrington family, who farmed at Upper Hareslade, could also be counted on for help. Father and son would help with the sheep, while Mrs Barrington used to love to provide some of her home made cooking to sustain the men on their long hard day's task. From High Pennard, Johnny Webb and Johnny Phillips were always eager to be part of the gang. The men who actually carried out the arduous task of washing were usually the four men from the

Construction of sheep pens, 1934.

Jones family; they were excused any of the other work involved in the process. One such task was the construction of sheep pens at the edge of the meadows bordering the river. Wooden gates and posts which were used for the purpose were brought down the cliff by horse and cart. The poles would already have pointed ends and would be hammered into the ground. The heavy wire fences would then be securely tied in. The 'washers' would wear their oldest clothes and boots; these would often be clothes that had been discarded and kept specially for this purpose. After the washing was complete they would dress in the clean clothes that they would have brought down with them. The old clothes would be completely ruined from the cold water which the men had had to stand in, up to their waists, for anything up to two or three hours. Arthur Jones tells how one man nearly drowned when a struggling sheep pulled him under the water; he had to be pulled ashore and given artificial respiration. The wool was washed by the men's hands repeatedly rubbing through the fleece and lifting it; this was a time honoured method which had been passed down from father to son. The ridge of stones provided the perfect clean place for the fleeces to drain and the sheep to dry off. The grease from the fleece would have

Sheep washing in Pwlldu Pool, 1936.

risen a quarter of an inch from the skin and this enabled the men to use the hand shears far more effectively.

When all the sheep had been safely penned prior to washing, the men would see Mary Phillips coming down the cliff from the Pennard side, with a large basket over her arm. Safely wrapped round with a small Welsh shawl, would be warm freshly baked Welsh cakes; these with sandwiches and hot tea would provide a welcome meal for the men.

The three men about to enter the water would also take a large measure of whiskey, safely carried in a small bottle, which would be tucked into a waistcoat pocket. With a twinkle in his eyes, Arthur Jones assured me that he had not forgotten his Band of Hope pledges, which he had signed with his father in 1909, but the spirits would be strictly for medicinal purposes, as it was very cold in the water! He did, however, admit that after some twenty minutes or so, the water would warm up, as the body heat from the twenty sheep or so that had been already dipped, would have been transferred to the pool.

After about three hours, when the washing was complete, the men would leave the water, get into a complete change of dry clothing, have another nip of whiskey, and eagerly await the sight of Mrs Barrington coming down the cliff from the Bishopston side, with yet another feast for the tired men. In the meantime, the sheep would be released and make their own way back to the farms. Arthur explained that because the lambs had remained in the farmyards, the sheep would know exactly which farm to head for. The terrain was very

Washed sheep returning home over bridge.

familiar to the sheep, as they often grazed on the cliffs and in a dry, hot summer would have made their own way down to the river in order to drink. Of course, mistakes did happen, sheep went missing, and false claims were made.

One of Arthur Jones' favourite tales about sheep washing is the day when the Hunts boys beat the Jones team to the washing pool! We know that at this time the valley was far more open, there were fewer trees and while walking down the cliff from the Bishopston side the opposite cliff would be in perfect view. Arthur Jones was about twelve at the time, his younger brother, Ivor, ten, both of an age to enjoy a race. As Arthur told me the story the excitement of the competition was still in his voice:

> *"Well you see – we had just started herding a flock of sheep down Moses Road from Bishopston, when suddenly from across the Valley a similar herd was being driven down the road from High Pennard by the lads from Hunts Farm, who used to use the same pool as us. A grand race started – down the cliff we sped, both making for the pool. Hunts managed to get there first – just by a head! We had to secure our sheep in one of our fields until the other flock had been duly washed. We didn't mind too much, as they weren't as fussy as us, so we knew they wouldn't be too long!"*

Before they had finished washing the sheep, a small boy who had run down the cliff from Hunt's farm, arrived with the news of the birth of a new son. The remaining sheep were quickly washed and all the Hunt's men went to Beaufort to '*wet the baby's head*'.

Shearing

It would take about three days for the sheep's fleece to completely dry out. It was essential that they did not get wet again, so the weather was watched with care, any sign of rain and the shearing would have to be postponed. In the early 1900's all shearing was done by hand as it had been for hun-

Mr David Jones (Sen) hand-shearing one of his flock.

dreds of years. Later, a hand shearing machine was used, which was quicker; two men worked the machine, one holding the clippers, while the other supplied the power by turning the handle of a heavy wheel. Some farmers were better at it than others. David Jones claims that he was no expert, and indeed he had many other essential jobs on the farm that still had to be done, even during shearing time. Even so, he was able to shear at least 25 sheep a day. The shearing took place in the open air, the pen holding the sheep was constantly moved onto new ground so that the whole process could be carried out in clean conditions. The fleeces were then stretched out and finally rolled up, with the tail being used to tie them. Placed in special huge sacks which held 30 or 40 fleeces, they would wait to be collected by a Mr Jones of Gorseinon. No fleeces would be accepted unless they had been washed.

Haymaking

Other work had to be done on the farm. Hedges had to be made stockproof, gates and gate posts maintained. But with-

Hareslade, 1920.

out doubt, the happiest and most sociable of these tasks, and always the most important, was making the hay which all the stock would need for winter keep. This was a time when young and old from the community helped for the sake of the company and the hearty meals! When the weather was set fair and the grass ready for mowing, the farmers, their sons and the many willing volunteers would go into the hayfield as soon as the dew had disappeared. In the early 1900's, the hay was cut by hand with scythes. David Jones remembers this time well,

> *". . . the old men with the scythes were so skilled it was a joy to watch them. There would be half a dozen of them cutting one field, working aslant downhill, and on reaching the bottom walked up again, whetted their scythes, and went down mowing the next strip in the same way. Once they got into the swing they had to keep going, they daren't get too near each other or one man would get cut."*

In fine weather the swathes were raked into long rows and left to dry. In a day or two, as the wilting grass lost weight, women, children, and even older residents would take up a long handled wooden rake and turn and toss it until it was 'made'. When ready, the hay was pulled into heaps along the rows and carefully built into haycocks, so that the rain could run off the surface. Finally, if the weather was fine, the lines of new sweet hay would be pitched up with forks onto a waiting wagon. I often helped with these tasks as a child, and like David Jones, remember it as *"a lovely time – we were all like one big family, the people of Pwlldu and High Pennard – everyone joining in."*

In the late 1920's horse drawn mowers were used. At this time David Jones (Sen) had purchased 52 acres of land near Pennard Church. His sons remembered the long day's toil involved in haymaking. They would leave Lower Hareslade at 4 a.m. and would reach Pennard, with the horses at 5 a.m. The early morning start, particularly on a hot summer's day was made as much for the horse's sake, as for the men. Two machines were used and three men employed. Each machine had a driver, while the third man's task was to sharpen the knives for each machine. They would finish one field about 9 a.m. before starting on the other. Carrying hay would then go on until 11 p.m. at night.

Rick building was especially skilled work, and sometimes the ricks would be placed in the corner of the fields that had been cut. Mr Ivor Jones remembered one such rick, that was a familiar sight in Pwlldu. The two Bridge meadows situated alongside the bridge, skirting the Bay, were known as excellent hay fields, and there was always a rick built in the corner of the field nearest the Bridge. If carefully built, they could withstand the winter storms and gales; a tarpaulin would sometimes be roped over the top to give extra protection.

Threshing

Corn, wheat, barley and oats would be cut with the horse drawn reaper and stacked in ricks in the fields. The wheat and barley would then be left for 10 or 12 days but the oats required at least three weeks in the fields. A good supply of oats was essential in order to give the horses the energy they needed to carry out the demanding jobs on the farm. During October and November, a traction machine would come

The traction machine visits a Bishopston farm.

around from Killay. This would visit all the farms in this area, starting in Bishopston, Backingstone and right round to High Pennard. A similar machine would visit all the farms from Mumbles to Manselfield.

As with hay-making the farms were never short of volunteers, and this was particularly true at Lower Hareslade, as David Jones remembers,

> *"We had so many volunteers that we had to send some people home – they even came from Parkmill. You see, they had all heard about my Mother's dinner – we used to have a magnificent spread, a full cooked dinner with a huge joint of beef and all the vegetables. This was in the farmhouse, all sitting round a long table, it was like a big party."*

Right up until the 1940's horses were used to carry out all the farm work – ploughing, harrowing, dragging loaded carts through mud and mire. These animals had to be fed, watered and harnessed, before the day's work could start. Nobody minded, least of all Mr David Jones. As he said *"You could talk to a horse"*. His father was well known for his knowledge of horses and his advice would be sought by many farmers

'A team of three' with David Jones and sister, Mary.

throughout Gower, who went to buy horses in the horse sales. These horses would not be heavy Shires, but a cross with a Welsh Cob. David Jones remembered his horses with affection, as he said:

> *"Horses are almost human and obey the human voice instinctively, knowing the farm work as well as his master. I had one horse that I was particularly fond of. He was a Welsh cob, or more of a Shire – a big, beautiful horse, by the name of Duke, – he had been a collier horse once. He stayed on the farm right up until I finished farming. We'd be planting out potatoes – I'd only have to say 'on top now, Duke' and he'd know that it was time to walk down the row and cover up the potatoes."*

Arthur Jones, remembering the time before farm hands drove heavy machinery up and down the fields, remarked to me – *"I often wonder what my father would say if he came back now. Do you know he'd probably say – 'Whatever became of the horses'?"*

Ploughing matches and Hedging competitions were eagerly

looked forward to by all the farmers. These started on the last Thursday in January and then took place on further Thursdays; the last match being held on March 1st. Mumbles and Gower Union District was the first show, followed by Lower Gower, Three Crosses, and finally Penllergaer. The horses would be there resplendent in their shining brasses, alas now only seen in museums or hanging around mock wooden beams in pubs!

Every Tuesday farmers from Bishopston or High Pennard would meet up to drive any stock that needed to be taken to Gowerton Mart. They would be driven right along the road to Kittle, Three Crosses and finally down to Gowerton, a journey that would take them anything between two, and two and a half hours. Those cattle that were being taken for slaughter would have an even longer journey. The agent, Robert Morgan from Three Crosses, would have already visited the farms and purchased the animals he needed. Often farmers in Bishopston and High Pennard would get together a small group of cattle and drive them across the cliffs to Pennard, where they might pick up a few more beasts. Killay Station was the meeting point and in order to get there the cattle would have to be driven right across Fairwood Common. At Killay there would usually be about 40 cattle waiting to be driven by one man and his dog, all the way along the road to Swansea, finally ending at the abattoir in the Hafod.

Shooting Parties

When the Gilbertsons were about to organise a shoot in Bishopston Valley, their chauffeur Rogers, was given the task of finding twelve or fourteen boys from the surrounding farms as beaters. This was a much prized job, as not only did it provide a day of excitement and fun, but each boy received five shillings, riches in those days! Only one or two boys were hired from each farm, so in the Jones family the brothers would have to wait their turn. There would usually be about five men on the shoot, all 'gents' from the family in Pontar-

Farmers Shooting Party in the Valley, c.1920.

dawe and bigger houses such as Fairwood. They would start at Great Kittle, cross over from Vineyards to the other side of the valley, work all the Pennard side, right down through Hunts Woods. They would finish at Paradise Meadow for lunch. The gentry would have their meal in the big house, while the beaters enjoyed their buckets of sandwiches and hot tea, which was served to them in the garage. When lunch was over, they would start at Vineyards and go down the other side of the valley as far as Pwlldu Bay. As Ivor Jones said, *"It was a lovely shoot, – it was a small shoot, but a hard shoot – very satisfying."*

There was no pheasant shooting after February 1st. This is when Mrs Gilbertson would give the farmers a day out shooting, but not pheasants! – only rabbits and pigeons. This was a day that Mr Harry Phillips, grandson of Johnny Phillips of Cliff Cottage used to really enjoy. Although tenants did not have the right to kill 'winged game' – pheasants and partridges – even if they invaded the fields, there is little doubt that the odd bird did find its way to the farmer's table!

It was not only the gentry who were able to enjoy a shooting party. At the beginning of the century, land was comparatively cheap and people from many walks of life used to buy

Ivor Jones of Knapp Farm.

it. One such person was a relation of Arthur Jones who owned some fields at High Pennard Farm; the present farmhouse had not been built at this time. The day for the shoot arrived and his uncle and friend invited Arthur to beat the bushes for pheasants. They walked around the cliffs to Pwlldu and called in Beaufort for a few drinks. As they left the pub and continued up the steep path to High Pennard, it became

David Jones of Hareslade.

obvious to Arthur that his uncle's friend was rather the worse for drink! They arrived at Bickin Field where the shoot was to take place. His Uncle Jack then told Arthur to go round one side of the field and help beat for his friend, while he would take the other side. At the end of the field there was a bit of a wood and one of the small trees was growing over a pit. Arthur was told to, *"Go over there boy and see if there's a pheasant in that bush."*

To Arthur's delight there was a huge bird sitting plumb in the middle of the bush. Just as he got ready to beat the pheasant out of the bush so that it could be shot while flying, to his great surprise the tipsy sportsman, who was afraid that he would lose face with his friend if he were to miss the bird, went up to the bush and shot him cleanly where he sat. He

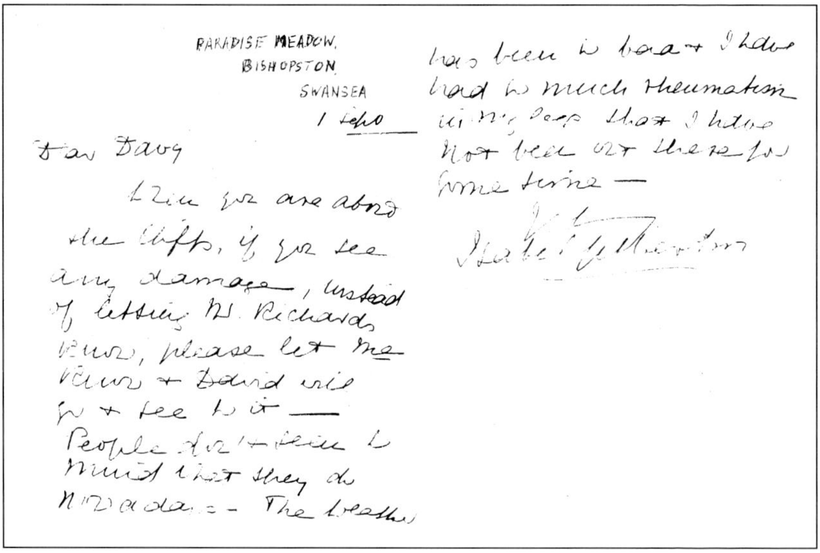
PARADISE MEADOW,
BISHOPSTON
SWANSEA
1 Sept[illegible]

Dear Davy

When you are about the cliffs, if you see any damage, instead of letting Mr Richards know, please let me know & David will go & see to it — People don't seem to mind what they do nowadays — The weather has been so bad & I have had so much rheumatism in my legs that I have not been out there for some time —

[illegible]
Isabel Gilbertson

Letters from two Lady Landowners: Mrs Gilbertson and Mrs Vivian

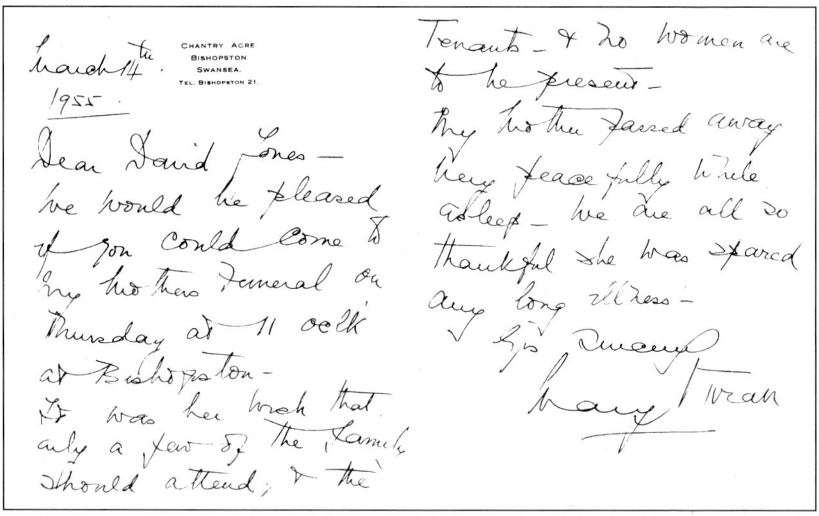
March 14th. 1955.

CHANTRY ACRE
BISHOPSTON
SWANSEA.
TEL. BISHOPSTON 21.

Dear David Jones —
We would be pleased if you could come to my Mother's Funeral on Thursday at 11 o'clk at Bishopston —
It was her wish that only a few of the family should attend; & the Tenants — & no women are to be present —
My Mother passed away very peacefully while asleep — We are all so thankful she was spared any long illness —

Yours sincerely
Mary Vivian

then turned to the young boy and made him promise, *"If your Uncle Jack asks thee, you say I shot the bird flying."*

In all my conversations with the tenants of the Gilbertson Estate, it was obvious that Mrs Gilbertson was held in great esteem. Her relationship with her tenants was exceptionally good. The Royal Commission in 1893, *"on the way that land in Wales and Monmouthshire was held, occupied and cultivated,"* stated that theoretically there was no need for the lease to be renewed by either landlord or tenant from one year to the next; thus farmers didn't have security of tenure. Most farmers didn't want it, particularly in places like Pwlldu and the surrounding area where there was mutual trust between landlord and tenant. Ivor Jones affectionately recalls Mrs Gilbertson as:

> *". . . a proper lady. She would often come down to the farm when I was farming at Knapp. She would stand watching the men at work in the fields for quite a long time. When I asked her if I could help her in any way, she would reply, 'No thank you, Ivor, I just love watching the men work. You know I don't make much money from my farms, but I do so love them'."*

When she realised that Ivor had four children and had to get all his drinking water from the spring in the Valley, she arranged for the main water to be brought to the farm. It would have cost him £780 to bring the water from Pyle, but Mrs Gilbertson agreed to pay the costs if he dug the trenches required; she even promised one of her estate workers to help him in his work.

David Jones also spoke of his happy relationship when he farmed at Lower Hareslade. He said that in some ways they felt like free-holders; they were readily given any permission for improvements and on the whole the rents were very fair; they were able to live happily and do the best for their farms. Further proof of this mutual respect, and genuine concern for her tenants, which I had seen with my own grandfather, is obvious in these letters lovingly kept by David Jones for many years. In the first letter Mrs Gilbertson expresses her concern that because of her rheumatism she has been unable to get out and make her customary inspection of the cliffs for any possible damage or rubbish left by tourists. Her letter affectionately addressing Mr Jones as 'Davy' and asking for his assistance, displays the excellent relationship they shared.

The second letter from her daughter, Mrs Hugh Vivian, was written just after her mother's death in 1955. Even at the end of her life Mrs Gilbertson thought of her tenants and made a special request that they should be at her funeral.

So the older generation look back on their lives and remember what fun they had and muse on whether their grandchildren, who have so many material possessions, and for whom life in many ways is a lot easier, enjoy life so much. Is this just nostalgia or were the simpler pleasures more satisfying? Certainly the little world of the Bishopston Valley, Pwlldu and High Pennard had provided them with security, a place in which they were born and brought up, a place they would never forget, a place which gave them many adventures in which they shared; it was a place that they belonged to and would remember all their lives.

The Landlords of Beaufort and their Customers

Although Gower folk have a reputation for 'keeping themselves to themselves' and not considering anyone as 'a local' until their family had lived in the village for several generations, they still welcomed visitors. Any strangers who were willing to enjoy their way of life and appreciate the glorious countryside they lived in, were welcomed as friends and never forgotten. Literally hundreds of such visitors came to Pwlldu, even during the period of the two world wars, and it was their custom that kept busy the pub at Beaufort and the tea rooms at Jenkins Cottage. Some of these visitors came from as far away as the Midlands; they would return year after year, loving the remoteness of the Valley, the splendid cliff walks, the safe sandy beach and the weird rock formations. They would return to the inn, where on cold days they could curl up in front of a log fire, or take a drink in the bar where often interesting, even eccentric characters would delight in regaling them with stories and anecdotes of the history of this unique valley. They would sometimes be joined by members of a shooting party, known locally as 'the toffs', who after a hard day's shoot would repair to Beaufort for a meal and a drink.

Then there were the day visitors. In Mumbles the two biggest livery stables were run by Presdee and Peachey. These companies would keep anything between thirty to forty horses and carriages; after all it was quite usual for a funeral to require at least forty horses. In the Spring and Summer these two firms would often use their bigger horse drawn carriages to carry anything up to 50 people out to the cliffs at Pwlldu, where they could enjoy such superb sea views. Pwlldu Lane was the same width as it is today, and only one carriage at a time could pass down its length. Luckily the drivers perched high on their seats could easily spy any oncoming coaches. There were several passing places in the lane where a patient driver could pull in when required. Arthur Jones remembered working in his father's fields as a small boy:

> *"People weren't in such a hurry then, and there was far more courtesy on the roads. And in any case everyone knew everyone else – I knew all the people from Mumbles, at least all the 'toffs' who used to come down the lane in their carriages. I'd be working in the fields, and I'd hear a cheerful voice shout out 'How's the potatoes, boys?' – then with a cheery wave of his whip the coach driver would pass on – oh yes, I knew them all. They could all see me as they were so high up they could see over the hedges and into the field."*

At the end of the lane, the passengers would dismount, enjoy the view for about fifteen minutes, and then get back into the carriage for the journey back to Oystermouth. On week-ends and particularly Bank Holidays many people would go right down into the Valley and sample food and drink from the Beaufort.

Mine Host: Mr Samuel Jones

After Aunt Jane's death in 1907, for a time, the pub continued to be run by members of the original Jones family. Mr Samuel Jones had four sons: William, John, George, and Thomas. There were also five daughters. John Jones was to marry Celina Gwynn, who was the sister of David Jenkins' wife, Matilda. So once again the two houses in the Valley were linked through marriage. Arthur Jones remembered how his grandmother used to serve teas and drink from the Malt House, which, of course, was no longer used to brew beer. Many of her customers were holiday-makers who came past the Malt House, on their way back from the beach.

Mine Host:
Mr Arthur Llewelyn Whapham
(the Rugby playing landlord)

After the Jones family left Beaufort, it was run by the Whapham family. Mine host was Mr Arthur Llewellyn Whapham and apart from the name gleaned from the licensing records, and a vague memory by some of the older residents of the Valley that he had been an 'All White' I could discover few details of his time at Beaufort. Then, as was to happen time and time again as I was writing this book, Fate intervened. My son's mother-in-law, who was a teacher in a Junior School in Cardiff, had spent a few days holiday with us at Beaufort. On returning to school in the Autumn, she found a new member of staff. Trying to make her welcome, she sat next to her during break and began to give her details of her Pwlldu holiday. Her new colleague suddenly interrupted her by asking "Do you mean the Beaufort, Pwlldu, on the Gower coast?" When she was assured that this indeed was the inn where the holiday had taken place, she calmly replied, "My mother was born there!" The lady in question was Mrs M. L. Winter, who was the grand-daughter of Arthur Whapham. Not only was I able to interview her, but I was able to actually bring both her and her sister, back to Beaufort, where they had been born. It proved to be a very emotional experience, as they sat in the garden, and remembered some of the fascinating stories of people who lived in Pwlldu Village early this century.

Arthur Whapham was an 'All White' – a well-known local rugby player, who never missed a game at St Helen's and would always walk home to Pwlldu after the matches. As one can imagine his bar was well patronised. Indeed his grand-daughter assured me that Beaufort, at this time, sold more beer than any pub in Mumbles. The pub had never been known to respect the lawful drinking times and continued to be open at all hours, even on Sundays. Most of the people of the valley felt they were above the law, even the local policeman who was a regular 'out of hours' customer.

One piece of legislation that was observed was the Welsh Sunday Closing Act of 1885 which stated that even if a public house was closed, a bona fide traveller, who was more than three miles from his home could demand food and drink, even on a Sunday. It is not surprising to find that many drinkers from Oystermouth could be found in Beaufort on a Sunday! The Clyne miners also made use of this legislation and joyfully walked down the Valley in order to enjoy a Sunday drink.

In 1914, the first year of the war, Molly Winter's father was a serving soldier, so she had come with her mother and two sisters to live with her grandparents at Beaufort. Her grandparents also had seven other children, all of whom lived at home, so once again the sleeping accommodation of Beaufort must have been stretched to the limit! In the true tradition of all Beaufort families, everyone was expected to help in the day-to-day running of the inn. By the last year of the First World war, Molly was only four years old, but she remembered well how she and her sisters were expected to help serve at tables, when the inn was full. The number of customers was further increased by soldiers who had been billeted at Beaufort; these men she remembered used to have their meals at long trestle tables placed on the lawn.

'Grampy' worked hard and expected everyone else to do the same. Beaufort was well run and everyone had their appointed tasks. The young maid who lived in the house, had to work very hard, and Arthur Whapham was quite strict with her. Her exhausting day's work included scrubbing the inn's floors, peeling vegetables, not to mention cleaning out the two earth 'privies' at the bottom of the garden, next to the pig sty. At 9 p.m. she was shut in her room and expected to stay there until the early hours of the next morning, when she must be ready to start her daily routine all over again. Molly remembered the young maid often escaped through her window (she apparently slept on the ground floor, just off the store room). On one occasion when she had climbed an apple tree, to steal some fruit, her long white night-gown got caught on some branches; her struggles only led to her being even more firmly held. It was several hours before someone from the Bar heard her cries and she was finally rescued.

Another memorable event was when the crew of a foreign ship, which had been wrecked off Worm's Head were brought to stay at the inn. Among the sailors was a very large black man. Young Molly had never seen a black person before, and this man was even more fascinating, as he had taken a great fancy to her grandmother, and insisted on following her around wherever she went, like a pet dog! This caused a great deal of amusement for the customers as her grandmother was a particularly tiny woman and was dwarfed by this huge black giant of a man.

Yet another crew was temporarily housed at Beaufort when a schooner was wrecked off the Needles. These men turned out to be very rough characters and frightened both the small girls. Some of the men used their wicked looking sheath knives to spear the food into their mouths, and on one occasion a particularly evil looking character threatened to cut out young Dorothy's tongue. She ran screaming upstairs and made sure she never went near them again, especially when they were eating.

Molly's earliest recollections that a war was going on was not so much the presence of the soldiers, but the untiring work of her beloved 'Grampy', who spent as much time as he could digging every inch of the garden where a large variety of vegetables were grown. When he was not digging, he was tending the fruit garden, feeding the chickens, or cleaning out the pig-sty, which was still used to house two pigs at the bottom of the garden. In addition there was a lean-to conservatory built onto the malt house where a wonderful crop of tomatoes was grown. The small girl was constantly being told that there was a war on and they had to grow as much food as they could

However he did take time off to build a summer house of bamboo on the side of the Malt House, the back of which was directly opposite Ship. This was a very popular place for the children to play, especially when the weather was inclement. (I was later to play in this very same shelter, with the Beaufort evacuees during the Second World War).

Arthur Whapham was a very popular landlord; he became a well-known Pwlldu character, who was something of an eccentric. One of the many things for which he is remembered, was his prowess at driving his specially built, beautifully sprung, light carriage. To pull this superior vehicle, he had purchased one of the 'Post' ponies. The Gower Mail team of horses had to be well bred and fast in order to carry out the long Gower run. When his beautiful pony was hitched to this superbly balanced gig, everyone had to get out of his way, so quickly did he travel. Word would quickly spread that Arthur Whapham was coming down Pwlldu Lane and the road would empty in a flash. All the farm-workers in the fields would cheer as he passed. Arthur Jones remembered one occasion when he took the Caswell bend so quickly that all the spokes of his wheel came out and clattered across the road!

Ham and Eggs

The first three decades of this century could well be called the 'Ham and Eggs' era. On a Bank Holiday, it was not unusual for many people to camp out in the valley over night; together with the day trippers, not to mention the 'regulars'; both Beaufort and Ship would be catering non stop to meet the demand. Hezekiah Jenkins related how his grandfather "*would be up to his waist in egg shells, after serving hundreds of customers*". Somewhat of an exaggeration, no doubt, but we do know that not only the two inns in the Valley served ham and egg teas, but that Webbs' Cottage was equally popular. A gang of young men in their 20's were regular visitors to Pwlldu and always finished their day's visit at the Webbs' for a ham and egg tea. Mrs Webb always referred to them as the 'Sketty boys'. One Sunday, after tucking into their favourite meal, they complained that the eggs were rather small. The quick response came, "*Ay boys, but they be tight!*"

Harry Phillips remembers his grandmother, Mary Phillips supplying teas at Cliff Cottage. In Beaufort, when the inn and gardens were full, they set up tables outside the Malt House and Arthur Jones' grandmother served there right through her teens. People could also bring their own food to eat and they would be supplied with tea and hot water. This steady stream of holidaymakers making their way down the cliff from the Bishopston side encouraged another piece of private enterprise. An old lady from Bishopston served ice-cream and lemonade from trestle tables that had been set up in the small lay-by, used as a passing place, half way down Moses Road. Brandy Cove was also being visited by more and more people and Mrs David Jones (Sen) used to take trays of hot water and tea out to the holiday-makers on the beach.

By the time Molly and Dorothy James were young girls, the first motor-driven lorries appeared on the track and supplies for the bar stores and coal were brought down in this way, but the beer continued to be delivered by horse drawn sledge.

Molly's two older sisters, Kathleen and Muriel James, worked in Swansea, and walked every day, whatever the weather, to Mumbles, where they caught the Mumbles train to Swansea. Often on their return journey, they would be heavily laden with extra provisions required by their grandmother. If the shopping was particularly heavy they would hire Old Peachey's hansom cab to take them home, but most days they walked round the cliffs from the pier. On one of these walks back to the pub, the two sisters were attacked by a ram which suddenly appeared on the track skirting Brandy Cove. Kathleen promptly threw a bag containing ten pounds of sausages directly at the animal, and the girls ran away as quickly as possible. Apparently the sausages were later returned by Mr Jones of Hareslade Farm who had found them on the path while out for an evening stroll.

One of the more bizarre incidents that occurred in Beaufort during these years was the making of a film. I was given the details of the occasion by Mrs Queenie Heath, who is actually now my daughter's mother-in-law!

The Director of the film was a Mr Leigh Jones, who owned

the Mackworth Hotel in Swansea, together with a number of London hotels. His home was in St James Gardens in Swansea and although he spent most of his time in London during the week, he always returned to Swansea for the week-ends. He was passionately fond of Gower and one of his favourite haunts was Pwlldu. Of course, being in the same trade as Arthur Whapham, he knew him well and arranged to bring a camera man and a cast of six beautiful young girls to Beaufort in order to make the film. Young Queenie was to be the star, and well remembers being taken to the top of the cliff in a luxurious motor-car – quite an event in itself in those days – and then walking with the rest of the girls and the camera crew down the cliff, and over the bridge to the inn. All the girls had been kitted out with striking white polo-necked jerseys and white pleated skirts. Among the rest of the cast was Queenie's sister, Muriel and her greatest friend, the youngest Whapham daughter, Avril. After a scene on the lawn where they performed quite an intricate dance, they were asked to change into bathing costumes which were of the very latest fashion and had also been provided by Mr Jones. By now the tide had gone right out and a lovely expanse of sand had been left. Here they were to be filmed speeding across the bay in two land yachts. The camera man was a Mr Ernest, a dentist from High Street. Although he was an amateur the film was of a high standard and even received a showing at the Swansea Empire. Unfortunately I have been unable to trace a copy of the film or any information as to its whereabouts. An interesting corollary to this story is that when we extended the roof of Beaufort, we actually bought 1000 slates from the old Mackworth Hotel which was being demolished. The two gable end windows with curved tops looking onto the cliff path, are also from the Mackworth Hotel. I can't help feeling that both Arthur Whapham and Leigh Jones would have approved.

Most of the water for the inn came from the river. Both the James sisters remembered how as girls they used to help fill up containers by stepping out onto a large flat stone just in front of the bridge, known locally as the 'dipping stone'. From here it was easy to reach the water. Empty beer casks were also placed at strategic places to catch the rain water from the roofs, which was used to supplement the river water.

The White Lady

Every old inn has its own ghost and Beaufort is no exception. Sightings of the White Lady have been reported regularly from 1860 right up to the present day. She has been seen 'walking' in the Valley, crossing the bridge, or even appearing in the house itself. Like all ghost stories, there are many different versions, and nobody seems to know the girl's identity. Some called her 'Rachel', and even linked her with Rachel Timothy who had lived in Pwlldy Cottage. Others seemed to think she was a serving girl from Beaufort, who had become pregnant and killed herself and her young baby. All accounts, however, do agree on the appearance of the said ghost; a young girl in her late teens, appears in a long white dress, apparently clutching a small bundle to her chest. Molly James certainly knew about the White Lady and described a very interesting incident that occurred when she was living at Beaufort:

> *"My late uncle saw her not long after the end of World War I. He was returning from work very late one night and saw her standing on the little bridge. He was so frightened he walked, wheeling his bike right through the river which was running very quickly, in order to reach the house without using the bridge. My grandmother met him at the door and claims she also saw the ghost; only by this time she was ascending the cliff."*

I, myself, have never seen the White Lady, but I have been witness to a very eerie experience connected to a sighting which happened in the 1970's, not long after we bought the Beaufort.

At the time we were renting out part of the house to summer visitors. On this occasion our guests were two people

A happy scene outside the newly named 'Beaufort Hotel', c.1918.

connected with the medical profession – a doctor and his dentist wife. They had spent one night at Beaufort and we had invited them to enjoy a cup of coffee with us on the following morning. When we politely inquired whether they had slept well, both exchanged strange smiles and the husband commenced a very intriguing story. First, he explained to us that his wife was psychic and often experienced strange phenomena. They had retired to bed and were quickly asleep. His wife however suddenly found herself awake in the early hours of the morning, and instantly aware that there was someone standing on the top of a wooden staircase that led directly into the bedroom. Looking carefully, she saw a young girl, in a long white gown, clutching a bundle to her chest! At first she thought it was one of the young girls who were sleeping in the house and to whom she had been introduced the night before. Then she was convinced it was a ghost. By the time she had woken her husband the figure had disappeared. This was not the end of the experience. Later the same night, the husband was awoken by a loud banging noise as if a heavy wooden door was swinging in the wind. The night was completely still. Taking a torch he went down the stairs to investigate. Nothing and nobody was there.

The incredible factor about this incident is that these people were complete strangers, not only to us, but to the area. It would have been impossible for them to have picked up any information about our ghost, and yet the details were remarkably accurate; also the location of the strange knocking sound was exactly where the old heavy wooden door to the cellar had once been.

Mr Arthur Whapham, like most of his customers, enjoyed drinking and was often in an inebriated state. On one such occasion he had taken an oil lamp into the cellars to search for fresh supplies of beer. He tripped, knocking over the oil lamp which started a serious fire in the cellar. Fortunately his son, Glyn Whapham, home on leave from the First World War, heard his muffled cries and managed to get him out and extinguish the fire before it spread to the rest of the house.

Molly Winter remembers her grandfather losing his licence

but not the exact year. As it had been throughout its history, the inn was open at all hours. Customers used to keep cups of tea on the tables, just in case a surprise visit was made by the law! The story goes that a certain local policeman in the area was most anxious for promotion. He spent the whole of one Sunday crawling down the cliff path and approaching the inn on his belly. A careful glimpse over the wall revealed a number of people sitting at the long trestle tables, supposedly drinking cups of tea; in actual fact the cups contained beer! He had heard that this was a ruse to avoid detection so he quickly entered the premises and caught the drinkers red-handed. Names were taken and a successful prosecution was brought. Among those who had been apprehended were several of the crew members of *S.S. Tours*, which had been wrecked in Hunts Bay in 1918 (see account later). These men had been staying at Beaufort, while attempts were being made to refloat the vessel. Beaufort did lose its license and this was a particular blow to Arthur Whapham as he was a strong drinker himself. Apparently the year after losing his license he had quite a serious drinking problem. After visiting pubs in Swansea he often had to hire Peachey's hansom cab to bring him home.

The deeds to Beaufort House reveal that after William Jones died in 1916, his share in the property was passed on to his niece and adopted daughter, Elizabeth Mary Jones, who in the same year married David Gronow of Kittle Farm. In 1919 a new lease was drawn up between Elizabeth Mary Gronow, referred to as the 'Landlord', and David John Bassett, a well-known Swansea Hotel Proprietor, who was called 'the Tenant'.

Mine Host: Mr Edmund Butcher

As Arthur Whapham had become disqualified from holding a license, David Bassett had to look around for a new landlord for Beaufort. In No. 10 Union Street, mine host was Mr Edmund Butcher, a highly popular and experienced victualler. David Bassett offered him the Beaufort, which for the first time became known as 'The Beaufort Hotel'. The blanked out sign can still be seen on the front wall of the house.

Mine hosts: Edmund and Grete Butcher.

Although I had been given the name of Mr Butcher by the Jones brothers and many other of the older residents of Pwll-du, for years I had failed to find anyone with a knowledge of him or his family. As we know, most of this history has been revealed by a series of almost incredible coincidences, and yet another link in the chain was to be forged in quite a remarkable way. My brother, home from Australia for a long vacation in Britain, attended an Old Boys Reunion in Dynevor school, and via a chance conversation with an old school friend was told that a Mr Eddie Butcher, whose father had kept the Beaufort immediately after the First World War, was living in Dinas Cross, near Lower Fishguard. I was able to go and see him at his home and was given not only some wonderful photographs that he still possessed, but some more fascinating information to add to the Beaufort saga.

His father had been born and brought up in London but had spent holidays in Wales and eventually came to live there. While he was landlord at No. 10, he lived in Mumbles. Then the chance to run Beaufort came up and Mr Edmund Butcher, his wife, Mrs Grete Butcher, a German lady from Hanover, and their three children, two girls and a boy, moved to Pwlldu in 1918. They were to stay in Beaufort for four years, after which they moved up the cliff to High Pennard where they stayed in one of the cottages until the end of 1924.

As Eddie Butcher talked to me about his childhood in Pwlldu it was obvious that it had not only provided the most wonderful memories, but the whole way of life had been so exciting that it had remained one of the most influential times of his life. Immediately he started telling me of his adventures, many familiar chords of my own childhood at Pwlldu were sounded.

> *"There was so much freedom – it was like Texas – real cowboy country – no police, not even very much adult supervision – my parents were too busy. We owned anything and everything; outsiders and visitors to the Valley had no rights. Even if they got into trouble on the cliffs because they insisted on using old dangerous sheep tracks, that was their fault. We children had little or no sympathy for them."*

None of the children ever wore shoes. Even walking to school up the rough cliff path, their shoes would be tied round their necks by the knotted laces and only put on outside the school gates. It was a long difficult route to Bishopston school, especially in bad weather. Eddie remembers how on a very windy day in order to prevent themselves being blown off the cliffs, they would have to hold on to the cliff face with their hands and their backs pressed to the rock as they rounded 'windy corner', the bend that still catches the wind even today. When they got to the top of the cliff and Bishopston they still had quite a walk around to the school which was at the head of the valley. Sometimes in Summer they could manage to go through the far more pleasant and slightly shorter path through the Valley. Unfortunately Eddie Butcher hated school and has the most unpleasant memories of the place and the staff who quite literally ruled their charges with a rod of iron; the cane was used often and he felt, with a certain sadistic pleasure. The one pleasant memory seems to be the games of cricket played on the sloping grass by the river and the shop opposite the school where they bought their sweeties. Eddie's sister was a great friend of the girl whose family owned the shop and quite surprisingly spoke Welsh. She did not learn much Welsh from the one hour lesson she received in school, but managed to pick up quite a lot of the language from her friend.

Eddie and his friends, the Jones brothers from Hunts Farm, were always having great adventures. One of the most exciting happened shortly after they moved into Beaufort. Although lorries had started to bring down some food provisions, the lemonade bottles were still delivered in a large horse drawn cart by Spooners Ltd. On one occasion just as the cart rounded the last bend before the straight run down to the beach, one of the wheels went over the edge and the whole contraption toppled down the cliff. Fortunately Mr Butcher managed to rescue the horse which was largely unhurt, and the driver jumped to safety. To the small boys' delight the 'pop' bottles were thrown far and wide into the furze which at that time of the year had grown very high. While the adults were tending the horse and the shocked driver, the boys were busy trying to devise a plan for retrieving the lost 'pop' bottles. It was not the lemonade they were interested in, but the tops of the bottles which had precious rounded glass balls which made first class marbles. They had a brilliant idea – if they set fire to the furze it should be easy to locate the bottles. At first they managed to keep the fire in check, but to their horror the blaze spread and before long the whole cliff was alight. Mr Butcher was horrified and did not believe the story that the boys had concocted, namely that picnicers were to blame!

In Mr Butcher's time there was more livestock kept in Beaufort than ever before. Immediately in front of the Malt House a long wire enclosure was built right up to the stone wall and this was the home for one hundred geese. Of course the river provided a perfect watering place for them, as we can see in the photograph.

At the appropriate time they were plucked and taken to Swansea Market where they were sold for a good price. Three huge pigs were kept; they were so big that the young Eddie used to love to ride on their backs. His father did not approve

Geese in Pwlldu River.

of this practice and always knew when his son had disobeyed him, as the pigs bruised very easily and after the small boy had been riding them the tell-tale marks were always clearly to be seen. White leghorn chickens were kept in a run built onto the side of the Malt House, and provided huge white eggs which were very popular and in much demand, both for the market and for Beaufort customers. The Malt House itself was kept as a stable where two horses were housed. Mr Butcher put in a small window in the top of the side wall in order to improve the ventilation. The Butchers joined their High Pennard neighbours in their trips to Swansea Market. Not only did they sell eggs, geese, rabbits, chickens and bacon, but also the breasts of starlings which had been shot and plucked, usually by the children. These breasts were considered a great delicacy and fetched 6d each.

The Gower ponies were often to be seen in the Valley, and the boys used to ride them bare back until the inside of their legs were red and sore. They would sometimes round up three or four of the best and take them up the track to High Pennard, across the cliffs by the narrow path, then on over the Common, dropping down to the Mumbles Road which at this time was not very wide – the four horses would take up the whole width of the road. At the Market the boys would sell them for five shillings each, which was a lot of money in those days.

Another incident which has remained in Mr Butcher's memory is the occasion when a small trawler was wrecked on the beach by a very heavy tide. The six men in the crew managed to get ashore and they tethered the boat to the iron ring that still protruded from the rocks since the time of the quarry. The children were strictly forbidden to go near the boat, and of course this is exactly what they did! In fact in a matter of days the boat had become their favourite play area and they explored it from one end to the other. During one of these sorties young Eddie saw a handle protruding from the deck. On pulling it he heard a sudden loud whooshing noise. Thoroughly frightened the children fled back to the house and told their father that the boat was moving off the rocks. On examining the vessel Mr Butcher found that his young son had inadvertently pulled the handle of the toilet on board; that was the first time that young Eddie had ever seen a flush lavatory!

One place in Pwlldu that Eddie remembers above all others, is the deep, clear pool formed by the river as it passes beneath

Plank bridge with broken railings.

the steep rock face before finally breaking through to the beach. On a beautiful sunny day, he would sit for hours watching the movement of the hundreds of huge trout, the sun reflecting all the colours of the rainbow from their glistening silver scales. With just a long piece of black thread and a bent pin he could easily catch half a dozen at a time. These he would take to his delighted father.

When the Butcher family first arrived at Pwlldu, the railings of the bridge were in a state of collapse. The people of the Valley decided to remove them completely. For a time the bridge remained as it had been in Schenk's time, just two planks of wood stretching across the water. Mrs Butcher, however, was aware of the danger for the children who might easily fall in the water, and she herself did not like using the bridge after dark, with nothing to guide her steps. Before long Edmund Butcher managed to replace the rails, and made such a good job of it that the bridge remained as it was until well into the 1940's when it was replaced by the present concrete structure.

Among the few occasions when the family could get together to enjoy themselves was on swimming expeditions. They took full advantage of living so close to the sea, and bathed whenever they could.

It might have been an idyllic life for the children, but it was grindingly hard for the parents, neither of whom had ever lived in such an isolated spot, cut off from even the most basic of amenities. Water for washing, cleaning and cooking still had to be fetched from the river; but apparently there was a natural spring which came out of the bank just upstream of the bridge, providing beautifully clean, clear water for drinking.

Mrs Grete Butcher was not happy in her new home. The hard life brought many frustrations. A wonderful cook, she would spend days preparing a variety of breads, tarts and cakes for the expected arrival of a charabanc of holiday makers who would be brought to the edge of the cliff and then walk down the track for a day at Pwlldu. If, however, the weather turned bad, the expected guests would not turn up, and several days work would have been to no avail. There was no electricity, so no refrigeration, the surplus food would have to be fed to

Swimming Party: Mr and Mrs Edmund Butcher with young Eddie.

the pigs. The children were still quite young, and unlike previous tenants of Beaufort, there was no large family to help out with the hard work of running a busy pub.

The Chantry Acre Estate had been built up during the 18th century by the Swansea lawyer, Iltyd Thomas, who estab-

The Butcher family at High Pennard in 1923.

Edmund Butcher's pony and trap.

lished eventually the family of Thomas of Hill House and Glan-Mor, Sketty. Miss Thomas of Glan-Mor married Frank Gilbertson of Pontardawe. In 1920, it was he who decided to build a new house in part of the estate which overlooked Bishopston Valley and Pwlldu. He called his new residence Paradise Meadow. Their only daughter, who had married a

Captain Hugh Vivian, also built a similar house about half a mile away; this house was known as Chantry Acre. Both these houses were unique in that they were built from special prefabricated pieces and then the thatched roofs were added. Their appearance in such a striking position at the head of the Valley was to bring about a remarkable change in the Pwlldu landscape. The families who lived there certainly contributed to the revenue of Beaufort, but this also meant more work for Mrs Butcher. Both houses held regular 'shoots' in the Valley; and would end the day at the inn expecting the usual sumptuous supper provided by Grete Butcher.

The bar was still very busy and popular with locals and visitors alike. One of the specialities of the house, remembered by Mr Billy Ace (brother-in-law of Alfred Jenkins), was a large tankard of mulled beer. A long taper, or even the hot poker from the glowing log fire, would be plunged into the pewter tankard of beer. This was particularly appreciated in Winter by the fishermen whose hands were still frozen from holding their rods for hours on end. Swansea tugs often came into the bay on the top of the tide, in order that they could scrape the bottoms of the boats. Before sailing away on the next tide, a brief sojourn at Beaufort bar was considered a necessity. The locals from High Pennard, particularly Johnny Webb, Bob Hughes and Johnny Phillips (Cliff Cottage) were 'regulars'.

Mrs Butcher did make one very close friend, Mrs Spooner, whose husband ran the well-known Swansea lemonade business. It is obvious from the many photographs of the two ladies together that this friendship must have meant a lot to Grete Butcher who still felt herself cut off and living 'at the end of the world'.

Even Mr Butcher was not happy; apparently he suffered occasional 'blackouts' and his general health was not good. So in 1922 the whole family left Beaufort and lived for two years in a cottage at High Pennard. In 1924 they left on a potato boat to Hamburg.

After the Butchers left Beaufort, the house was taken over by Molly James's paternal grandparents, Mr and Mrs Samuel Jones from Norton. The licence was not applied for.

Mine Host:
Mr William John Whitehead

From the house deeds we know that in 1921 Mr D. J. Bassett made a new lease for the pub to the South Wales Public House Trust Ltd. which was for the residue of the term of 28 years from December 25th, 1919. This company in 1926 renewed the licence and put in Mr William John Whitehead as the landlord. The same year the ownership of the property was transferred from Mrs Gronow to Mr Frank Gilbertson, who as we know had recently come to live at the top of the Valley; indeed Beaufort was directly in the view from his house, Paradise Meadows.

After his retirement Mr Whitehead's son George lived in a bungalow in Pennard and it was there that I was able to talk to him. The family had always had close connections with Pwlldu. His great grandfather, Sam Rees had been the chief overseer of the Pwlldu Quarry. His Mother was the daughter of John Webb and had been born in Webb's Cottage, which at the time was a small farm and becoming famous for its ham and egg teas. There was one long field which was ploughed, while the other two fields were used for hay, which was used as feed for the horses. The woods which skirted the back of the fields also belonged to the property, but his grandfather had sold them to Mr Gilbertson, who wanted the woods for his shooting parties.

His father kept the pub for eight enjoyable years. As he and his wife were local people Pwlldu was not that remote to them and they enjoyed the clientele; as Mr Whitehead said, *"they were a nice class of people."* In Summer the pub was particularly busy, and there was a steady stream of summer visitors who continued to enjoy their teas served on trestle tables on the lawn as they had been for many years. The families from the Midlands and other places who had started to stay in Beaufort during the years that Mr and Mrs Butcher had run the inn, continued to book their holidays at Pwlldu and one or two of the five bedrooms were constantly let to visitors. By the late 1920's more and more people were enjoying the beach and in a good summer there used to be quite a crowd of people lining the shore. Many of these would call into Beaufort for a drink and something to eat before returning home.

The shooting parties continued to use the valley. Mr Gilbertson would advise Mr Whitehead when a shoot was to take place, and an order would be put in for sandwiches and cheese for the beaters; and instructions for a lunch to be prepared for the *'big toffs'* who would eat and drink before continuing back up the valley to Paradise Meadows where at the end of the day the shoot would end. This meal usually took place in the long tea-room which ran the whole width of the house, facing the sea.

Mr George Whitehead was able to give me a good description of the pub as it was in the 1920's and 30's. From the photographs we can see there were always two entrances; these would lead respectively into two bars. The entrance opposite the Jenkins cottage, which led via a stone built porch, to the best bar or lounge bar, as it was called, was used by holiday visitors and the gentry from Paradise Meadows and their guests. A doorway from the bar led into the tea or supper room where meals were taken. The other bar, which was entered through the garden and past a wooden porch (still there today) was the 'spit and sawdust' bar, for the locals and any regular customers. This was the bar where characters such as Bob Hughes would regale their listeners with tales and anecdotes. Bob had been wounded in the Battle of the Somme and had some wonderful war stories to tell.

Some of the local farmers were still regular customers, and of course at sheep washing time, many of the men would in time-honoured tradition, end the hard day by drinking hard all night. Often the drinking population would be increased by the presence of fishermen; and many small fishing and sailing

A 'toff' and a pig outside Beaufort, c.1920.

vessels would come into the bay, some even being beached in order to carry out renovations such as scraping the bottom or even painting. At such times the crews would inevitably find their way into Beaufort for drink and food.

Apparently many of the men in the bar would swear they had seen the 'White Lady, but as Mr Whitehead said,"*When the chaps had had a couple of pints they'd see all kinds of things!"* Some of them were convinced that the ghost was Rachel, and they did not like to pass the ruins of the cottage late at night.

Mr Whitehead's father was not a man to sit around the house and spent most of his time in the garden. Many of his farmer customers would bring him sacks of seed potatoes and as he hated to waste anything they would all find their way into the garden. The result was a bumper crop of potatoes – far more than they would ever need, so most of his customers would receive a bag of potatoes to take home! The chicken house was still used and eggs were plentiful; but the ham for the ham and egg teas had to be brought in because they did not keep pigs.

The road from Bishopston continued to be fairly rough, but the Star Supplies Ltd which was a company that owned a big old Ford van, did venture down the cliffs with essential goods. These were stored in the Malt House which was no longer a stable but simply known as 'the Stores'.

By now, the brewery was using a lorry with solid tyres to deliver beer. This vehicle could only carry the beer as far as the first bend in Moses Road. After this point the track became a sheer slope of shale which was highly dangerous for any form of wheeled vehicle. So once again the slide car was brought into service. The horse would take the empty sledge up to the

A flooded Valley.

bend where the beer barrels would be loaded and securely roped onto the sledge. Mr Paul Jones of White Knight farm remembers it well:

> *". . . chains would be fastened to the sledge and to the horse which would take up position behind the sledge; men and beast would take up these chains and use them as a brake to prevent the heavy load sliding too quickly down the cliff. Once at the inn, the beer was unloaded and the sledge reloaded with empty barrels, which the horse would take back up the cliff to the waiting lorry."*

The river continued to supply all the water needed by the inn. At certain times of the year, the river would often flood but the water rarely came further than the garden gate. However there was one exception; it happened when the weather had been particularly violent and heavy rain had been falling for several days. The sea was exceptionally rough and huge waves had thrown the pebbles into a cliff of stones, completely blocking off the flow of water to the beach. As the water rose, it not only entered the garden of Beaufort, but actually came under the door of the bar a couple of feet deep, causing dismay and consternation among the drinkers, *"We are doomed, we are doomed!"* cried many drunken voices. The bridge was under water, the whole of the floor of the Valley was flooded and the area between the beach and the cliffs became one vast lake. Apparently many men had to leave by the front door and take the path on the Pennard side of the cliff, and those who did not live in High Pennard had a long walk home over the cliffs. On the same occasion eight sheep were trapped on an island of land in the middle of the river; they were drowned before they could be rescued

Mine Host: Mrs Ada Bagge

When the Whitehead family left Beaufort in 1935, members of the Whapham family returned. Mr Arthur Whapham's eldest daughter, Mrs Ada Bagge and her husband Maurice took over the licence and the pub continued for a few years until 1939, when their son Terry, lost his life early in the war, and they did not have the heart to continue.

In 1937 the South Wales Public House Ltd had surrendered the lease to William Hancock and Company Ltd., and they in their turn, in 1939 surrendered the lease to Mrs Isabel de Winton Gilbertson (Frank Gilbertson having died in 1932) This is when the Beaufort Arms ceased to be a public house and became known as Beaufort House.

Beaufort Tea Rooms

Members of the Whapham family still kept their connection with Beaufort; Molly James' aunts, two sisters, Misses Ruth and Maude James continued to run a tea-shop at the house. They lived there for many years, until well after the Second World War, and became much loved Pwlldu characters, known to many (including me!) as Aunty Ru and Aunty Maud. These two ladies still took in summer visitors, but there were other strange members of the family living in the house.

Maud James was married to a man twenty-five years younger than herself. He was mentally handicapped and she said she married him in order to look after him. As children we used to play with him on the lawn; he was an odd child-like character but quite harmless. Ruth James had had a very sad life. In her teens she had become engaged, but for some reason the love affair finished and she never really got over it. Later in her life there was a much older man who wished to marry her, but she refused. Apparently he was devastated and committed suicide by hanging himself in the house.

There was a third sister Lydia, who lived at Beaufort all her life, but was very rarely seen. Early in her life, she became engaged to a sailor. Apparently he was always at sea and the wedding never took place. Then his boat sank in Swansea Bay and he was drowned. From this time on, she became a recluse. I vaguely remember seeing her at the window of the house, but I never met her, and indeed I don't think anyone ever did. When she died, Aunty Ru found a huge trunk in her bedroom, which contained her entire trousseau – twelve of everything.

The years rolled on. I had been to college, got married and had my first baby in 1955. Alison was born in June and it was a scorchingly hot summer. We wanted to spend all our days on the beach, but it was too hot for a young baby and where would I leave her when I went swimming? This is where the James sisters came to the rescue. They put the upstairs sitting room at my disposal, and this is where I could feed my new baby and admire the magnificent view from the huge bay window. I could then safely leave the baby in the garden under the shade of the apple trees, while I could return to the beach for my swim. All that long hot summer of 1955 we were frequent visitors to Beaufort and Aunty Ru and Aunty Maud became much loved adopted aunts. Little did I realise that one day I should be living in the house, helping to feed my new grand-daughter in the very same room, looking out at the very same view!

Ship or Jenkins Tea-room

David and Matilda Jenkins outside the Tea-Rooms with their eldest son, William, c.1910.

From the turn of the century and for as long as the Jenkins family remained in the cottage it was simply referred to as 'Jenkins' or 'Jenkins' Tea-shop' for that is what it became. David Jenkins and his wife, Matilda, kept it in the early 1900's. As the years went on, all the children, except the youngest son, Alfred Jenkins, left home and went their own ways. After Matilda's death, David, by now an old man much troubled by arthritis, was quite ready to leave Pwlldu and live with his family at Marmount House in Bishopston. He was still a much loved Pwlldu character and many of the older residents remember seeing him walking down the cliff to see his son. He was easily recognised by his long beard and the two sticks he used to help him down the steep path. He was known by all as Uncle David Jenkins. When he left Alf and Mary Annie to run the tea-rooms, he promised them that they could live in the cottage for the rest of their lives. The tea rooms continued to be very popular, and Mary Annie (or Marion as she became known) was as well-known as her predecessor for her Welsh or Gower specialities, such as *teisen lap*, scones, dowset and Welsh-cakes. They also kept a very small shop where you could buy a variety of highly coloured, and often rather stale hard boiled sweets and chocolate. Bottles of lemonade were available and a very lurid bright orangeade that was made with crystals and spring water, drawn from the same spring situated just above the bridge, that Eddie Butcher remembers so well. These were the things we bought as children in the 1940's, and I am assured by older residents that they were exactly the same in the 1920's and 30's.

Harry Phillips was postman for this area and remembers the Jenkins well. On a hot summer day after descending the cliff from Bishopston, he always tried to have some liquid refreshment before undertaking the long climb up to High Pennard. He would often meet Alf, with his green enamel water container tucked under his arm. If he had just fetched some deliciously cold spring water, the weary postman would be offered some. Harry remembers the Jenkins as:

> *". . . a lovely couple. They were very particular about their post – 'See that you put my letters straight into my hands' Alf would say."*

David Jenkins was known by everyone to be a keen fisherman. He owned a small fishing boat, but his main claim to fame was as a champion crabber.

An early document 'Acknowledgement of Trespasses on Rocks and Lands at Bishopston and Pennard' dated 27th May, 1732, has as one of its signatories one John Jenkin, almost certainly of Pooldie House. He was required to pay sixpence to his Lord for having *"severally catched crabs and lobsters in the*

Fishing at Pwlldu – Schenk, 1907.

rocks and the salt sands". So it is not surprising that David and Alf Jenkins were known as expert crabbers.

The Art of Crabbing and Lobstering

Until about 1880, this was not considered much of an industry. Before this date people like David Jenkins did go crabbing, but it was for their own consumption, and for friends and neighbours who lived near them. It was not until road surfaces had been greatly improved and the first horse bus service was run, that produce could be got to the Swansea hotels and particularly the market. Although the first motor bus services for Gower began in 1909, they were of little use to the residents of High Pennard, Pwlldu or even Bishopston, as none of them came via the village, because of the very steep Kittle hill; instead they ran over Fairwood Common. However we know that the Jenkins had a lovely little pony and trap, which David Jenkins used to take a regular supply of produce into Swansea; no doubt this would include crabs and lobsters, and fish that he regularly caught from the small fishing boat which was one of his most prized possessions. In 1918, a twice weekly

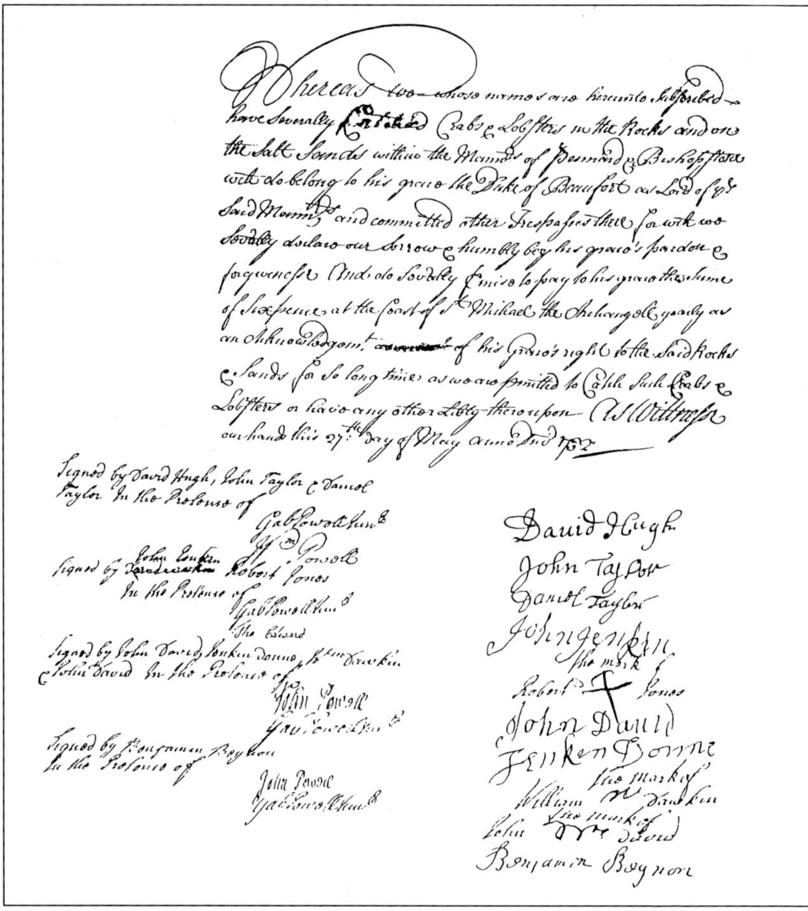

Whereas wee whose names are hereunto subscribed have severally Catched Crabs & Lobsters in the Rocks and on the Salt Sands within the Mannors of Pennard & Bishopston which do belong to his grace the Duke of Beaufort as Lord of ye said Mannors and committed other Trespasses there for which wee severally declare our sorrow & humbly beg his grace's pardon & forgiveness And do severally promise to pay to his grace the sume of Sixpence at the feast of St Michael the Archangell yearly as an Acknowledgment of his Grace's right to the said Rocks & Sands for so long time as we are permitted to Catch such Crabs & Lobsters or have any other Liberty thereupon. Witness our hands this 27th day of May anno Dni 1732

Signed by David Hugh, John Taylor & Daniel Taylor In the Presence of Gab Powell Junr, Wm Powell

Signed by John Jenkin Robert Jones In the Presence of Gab Powell Junr

Signed by John David, Jenkin Downe, Wm Dawkin & John David In the Presence of Jno Powell, Gab Powell Junr

Signed by Benjamin Beynon In the Presence of John Powell, Gab Powell Junr

David Hugh
John Taylor
Daniel Taylor
John Jenkin
Robert (his mark) Jones
John David
Jenkin Downe
William (his mark) Dawkin
John (his mark) David
Benjamin Beynon

'Acknowledgement of Trespassers on Rocks and Lands at Bishopston and Pennard', 27th May, 1732.

bus service, on Wednesdays and Saturdays, between Bishopston and Swansea was introduced. Finally in 1921, Isaac Jenkins started the first daily bus service from Bishopston into Swansea. This was too late for David Jenkins to take advantage of, but it was ideal for Alf Jenkins.

Regular crabbers, such as David Jenkins, reckoned they had a right to their own crabbing ground, and they closely guarded any details of their favourite holes and pools. Poach-

David Jenkins (Jun.) with his catch.

ing was not encouraged. When one man died, another member of his family would take it over. This was exactly what happened in the Jenkins family. From the time he was a young boy, Alf had gone along the shore with his father and been shown the holes to fish and the best equipment to use. By the time I knew him he was regarded as a star crabber and had built himself up quite a business, supplying numerous hotels and guest houses, and delivering regular supplies to Swansea market twice a week. He did not always use the bus but quite often, especially in good weather, he would walk around the cliffs to Mumbles carrying a cockle basket on his head loaded with some 30 or 40 crabs.

I had often watched Alf make his own crab hooks. I remember him telling me that the best hooks could be made from the tang of an old scythe blade, as hardened steel was the best material to use. Other times he would use thick wire. The hook had to be bent to an exact angle in order to get behind the crab or lobster and hook it out; if it was too rounded or sharp, the shell might be damaged. He sometimes made the long wooden handles out of bamboo, although others would be lovingly shaped out of any suitable driftwood that came to hand. On a good Spring tide when he could work for longer hours, and more holes would be revealed, he would often fill a small sack with some 30 or 40 crabs and always two or three lobsters. Sometimes his catch would be gone before he got home, as he would often meet up with some walkers or visitors as he was coming back from Hunt's bay, and they would be only too delighted to buy his catch from him.

As children we often used to try and follow Alf as he strode over the rocks in his sturdy army boots. The weather would have little or no effect on him. Dressed in old moleskin trousers, he would wade into the deepest gullies, the water often coming up to his waist. Plunging his hook deep into a familiar hole, by some subtle vibration of the rod, he would know if its resident was at home. It was almost impossible to keep up with him, as he visited three or four holes in so many yards. We would scramble over the rocks behind him, ducking down quickly to be out of sight should he glance our way. If he did catch sight of us, he would increase his pace and soon be lost to sight. When he did finally get back to the bay with what was obviously a heavy catch slung over his shoulders, he would still deny that it had been a good haul, and to the question *"Any luck today?"* the reply would always be the same, *"Not bad, just a few."*

He told me that he always knew where the best holes were by taking bearings from certain features of the cliff or some special rock formations. I found this hard to believe, perhaps because I couldn't do it myself, all the locations that I thought I had so carefully remembered seemed to merge into one. I was even tempted to go out and mark all the holes I had seen him visit with a cross painted in red paint! It was the same with the little crabbing advice he would sometimes grudgingly give us after a lot of persuasion:

> *"You can always tell if a crab is in the hole by the sound of his shell against the rock . . . a lobster is different, he's usually in a large pool so he's got plenty of room to manoeuvre . . . don't forget he moves very quickly backwards, watch your bare legs. Never get excited when you see a lobster, just put your hook behind him and coax him to the side of the pool where you can grasp him round the middle behind the claws."*

Chance would be a fine thing! Dad would be home on leave and I so wanted us to have a good catch, but oh the agony and frustration as we answered my Mother's question *"Got anything today?"* with a negative shake of the head or at best *" – just a few small ones."* Why couldn't we all be like Alf Jenkins?

Alf Jenkins (Mr Jinks) and Mary Annie Jenkins (Marion or Ma Jenkins)

Alf Jenkins in his youth was a tall, upright man, known for his spare good looks. He, usually had a cigarette clenched in the corner of his mouth, often took snuff, chewed tobacco, and was rarely seen without his flat cap pulled firmly on his head. He was a familiar figure to all the residents of the area,

Bathing Party from Ship. Back: Rosslyn and Dorothy Stephens.
Front: Emily Stephens and Mary Annie Jenkins.

as he strode across the cliffs. Everyone knew that he was courting a beautiful young girl who lived in Swansea; this, even at this time, was quite unusual as most young men and women found their future partners from the young people of the area. Mary Annie Morgan had first met Alf when he had delivered vegetables to a greengrocer's shop immediately opposite her home in Western Street. He always said that it had been love at first sight and indeed they remained all their lives, totally devoted to one another, perhaps even more so because there were no children.

Not surprisingly she faced great opposition from her parents, particularly when she announced that she was going to live in Alf's home at Pwlldu. Her Mother apparently told her that she would not last for one week in that God forsaken place miles from anywhere. In fact she was to live there until she was 83 years old.

The growing population of Swansea, together with the improvement of roads and transport generally, led to a thriving Market Gardening Industry in Bishopston, Pwlldu, and High Pennard. This was particularly true in both World Wars when,

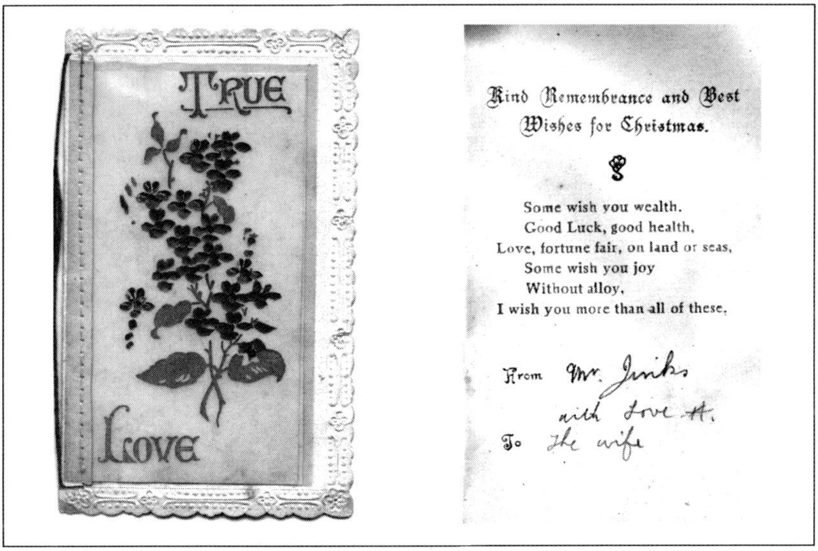

An early Christmas card.

as we know, everyone was encouraged to go flat out for production. The good soil, and absence of any late frosts, encouraged the farmers of the area to grow early market crops which could prove very profitable. Alf Jenkins was one such grower. Every inch of the moderate sized garden, located immediately behind the cottage, was planted with a large variety of vegetables and fruit. The garden was his pride and joy. Of course, like all gardeners in a country area, it was a constant battle against the ravages of birds and animals, especially rabbits. His fruit trees: red and black currants, gooseberries and raspberries were protected by a huge cage, which he had constructed from pieces of fisherman's net washed up by the sea. This would be reinforced with criss-cross bands of fishing line. Around the perimeter of the plot he constructed a sturdy wire fence, which he sunk a foot or more into the ground; this did deter most of the rabbits.

During the 1930's the discovery of new potatoes had been made, and these were in great demand. Alf quickly found that the sandy soil of Pwlldu provided ideal growing condi-

Alf Jenkins with his tomato crop.

tions. He was particularly proud of his chitting box which he had constructed from pieces of driftwood. Two varieties he was particularly fond of growing were 'Home Guard' and 'Red Royal'. He was known to be a good business man and would carefully gauge the market prices, so that he could sell his potatoes when prices were at their highest. He regularly sold a wide variety of produce in Swansea market, not only vegetables, but wild mushrooms, rabbits and of course his shellfish. He also did a very brisk trade in laverbread.

Laverbread

Shortly after her arrival at Pwlldu, Ma Jenkins learnt how to gather the black seaweed off the rocks from Hunts to Seven Slades. By the time I was old enough to take notice of what she was doing, she had become an expert at producing a high quality of laverbread and delivering it to many families in the area. This very popular edible seaweed has been eaten by Welsh country folk for many years. The actual weed is dark brown when found on the rocks, and its Latin name is Porphyra. Its black, rather slimy appearance after being boiled does make it seem rather unappetising. However when made into small cakes and covered in coarse oatmeal, it makes a delicious accompaniment to fried bacon.

The weed once collected, would be brought to the back kitchen in sacks. First it had to be washed thoroughly, at least three or four times. Remembering that all the water had still to be carried from the river, it is little wonder that it was such a long and tedious task. When I was older, I was allowed to help her, and I well remember how even after three washes we would still find small balls of sand sticking to the weed. After she was finally satisfied that all the sand had been removed, the weed was transferred to a huge black iron cauldron which had been greased with a lump of lard. The pot was then put on the range and the laver boiled for two or three hours. While boiling, a clean white cloth was placed over the top. This was to absorb the water. At intervals it was squeezed out, and rinsed in cold water, before being returned to the pot. This procedure kept the laverbread dry while cooking. When cool the weed would be placed on a large oak plank, over two oil drums (all booty from Davy Jones locker!) and chopped into fine pieces with the aid of two lethal looking knives – needless to say I was not allowed to help with this part of the process!! Miss Rosslyn Stephens told me of a very interesting method of cooking the lava, which was not done for commercial production, but was very popular with women who cooked the weed for private consumption. When the lava was placed in the large pan, prior to boiling, a layer of salt bacon was placed on top until the whole pan was full of alternate layers of bacon and lava. During the chopping process the weed and the bacon would be chopped together, giving a wonderful flavour to the finished product. In the 1950's it became more and more difficult to find the weed on the beaches, and this is when Alf went to Cornwall to secure extra supplies of the lava. He arranged for the raw seaweed to be sent to High Street station by rail, where he would be waiting to collect it.

Alf was not the only person in the area to make money from laverbread. There were a number of families in Bishopston and Murton involved in laverbread manufacture and indeed this area became known as the centre for the trade in Gower. One such family was the Gwynns, and Ivor and David Jones knew them well. Apparently on a visit to London, one of the sons was asked what line of business he was in, and on replying *"I'm a laverbread merchant"* was met with blank stares, nobody in London had ever heard of it! The Gwynn family also had laver sent up from Cornwall and Ivor Jones told me that although they had traded with these people for forty years, they had never met.

Yet another surprising enterprise was the selling of ice-cream. Billy Ace remembered Alf taking delivery of ice at the top of the cliff, then taking it down to the cottage, where ice-cream would be made in a large wooden churn which was turned manually with the aid of a long handle.

All these activities helped to augment the income from the Tea Shop which was still flourishing, especially in the Summer when the Valley was still attracting visitors. In fact business became so good that in 1935, Billy Ace and his father were asked to build on a glass tea room to the side of the cottage. Here at least six long trestle tables could be set up. At particularly busy times, members of the family who were living in Bishopston used to come down and help. Mrs Dorothy Davies and Miss Rosslyn Stephens remember going to Pwlldu, when their mother would be helping with the teas. They still remember being sent to fetch a can of milk from Knapp Farm, which they then desperately tried to stop spilling as they ran down the steep path, through Pwldwy Woods, back to the cottage.

Ma Jenkins had quickly become a much loved and admired member of the community. At this time she kept three dogs; two Airedales and a Pom. She became a familiar figure as she walked her dogs around the cliffs. Many people who knew her well, have remarked on her brilliant blue eyes, which kept their colour right up to the day she died. Another remarkable feature was her quite beautiful speaking voice, low, warm and always welcoming. The couple's popularity ensured the success of the tea shop. The landlords of Beaufort all loved the Jenkins. Although Alf appeared quiet and rather reserved, I was assured by Mr Butcher and Mr Whitehead that he could be great fun especially when he had a bit of 'pop' in him. He was much in demand in the Beaufort bar when not only could he tell many tales about his family's early history, but could play the concertina quite brilliantly. Apparently the Jenkins themselves used to celebrate Christmas with a party and the young couple would dance all night. The shop was never very successful and stock did tend to go stale. In the winter, when trade had all but disappeared, Ma Jenkins used to make up bags of all the left over sweets and give them at Christmas time, to any children she knew.

Collecting wood to feed the open fire in the parlour and the fire in the range, used for cooking, was a full time job, and one that fell to Ma Jenkins, Alf being too busy with his many projects. There is no doubt at all that Ma had a very special talent for not only finding wood, but with the aid of wedges and a long handled hammer, she was able to cut up the longest, heaviest, log of wood into pieces that could be easily carried

A young Mary Ann with one of her many dogs.

Alf Jenkins in his later years
– from a painting by Sheila Edwards.

back to the cottage. These logs would give free heat for many hours. One of my earliest memories of Ma Jenkins is seeing her sitting astride a huge log and in her deep musical voice saying, *"Wait, it'll talk to me now."*

Then with careful precision she would knock the wooden wedges into exactly the right position. Sometimes she would even leave them in the wood until the next day, or at least for a few hours. On her return the wedges would have done their work and with a few deft blows of the hammer, the huge log would fall into several pieces, a perfect size for burning. Even in later years, when she was quite an old lady she would still be out collecting driftwood, usually followed by two or three of the huge number of cats that she had collected after the death of her dogs.

My husband on seeing her still wielding a heavy hammer would offer his help. With a little smile she'd hand over the hammer and wedges and watch him struggle for a while, then she would politely take the hammer back, remarking, *"it's a bit too difficult for you, I'm used to it, see–."* She was in her seventies at the time!

All of their lives the Jenkins would have to carry all their provisions from Swansea, by foot down Pwlldu Lane and then down the rocky road to the cottage. They were extremely independent and although in their later years they received many offers of help, they always insisted on carrying their heavy bags, either on their own, or between them, with the aid of a handkerchief slotted through the handles of a huge canvas shopping bag; as one of their great nieces said, *"They were like a pair of pack horses!"*

Alf's tall, spare frame, belied a very strong constitution. The only time he was ever ill was when he went into hospital in the 1920's to have his appendix out. However, as the years went on, he became quite frail, and this led to a bizarre accident. The old couple were climbing Moses Road in order to catch the bus from Bishopston to Swansea, for their usual Friday trip to do some shopping. On such occasions, Alf would take the opportunity to visit some of the pubs in Swansea; Beaufort no longer having a license, Alf sadly missed being able to go next door for a pint. It was a cold day, with a strong wind blowing right into the Bay. He was wearing his long mackintosh which nearly came down to his ankles. As he reached Windy Corner, an especially strong gust of wind got under the mackintosh, filling it like a kite; his frail body lost its balance and he fell over the cliff. Amazingly, he was not seriously hurt, and although very shaken, insisted on continuing to Bishopston and catching the bus to Swansea. It was his precious day out, and it would take more than an accident to stop him enjoying it!

Alf's death in 1968 could not have been more appropriate for a man who had worked hard all his life, and from all accounts continued to do so until the night of his death. He died from a heart attack, quite peacefully sleeping in his own brass bed, which had been his parents and grand-parents before him.

Everyone who had known the devoted couple expected Mrs

Mrs Jenkins outside her cottage.

Jenkins to go into a decline and quickly follow her husband. This did not happen. For five years she managed on her own, still living at the cottage with reputedly 26 cats for company. She still collected water from the river, still collected her own wood from the beach, still went to Swansea for any necessary provisions, carrying them home on a little hand truck made from two pram wheels, and wood she had collected from wreckage off the beach.

She hardly changed in appearance; the deep blue eyes remained as blue as ever; the rosy red cheeks, lovely complexion, and above all the musical speaking voice. In some strange way she became even more a part of Pwlldu. All the regular visitors to the Bay would call at the cottage often bearing gifts of home made cakes. She accepted everything and everyone with the same winning smile. It is no wonder that she declared that she was never lonely.

By this time we had bought Beaufort and were often living there. Our offers of help were largely refused; she still valued her independence. However there was one occasion when she asked my husband if he could help repair a bolt on the back door. He duly bought a new lock and quickly had it fixed. She insisted on paying him for the materials used. Looking into her purse, she found she had no small change, *"Never mind, my dear, I'm sure Alf will have something."*

With a sense of growing apprehension my husband watched her climb the steep wooden stairs to Alf's bedroom above. Footsteps overhead, and then she returned triumphantly clutching some money in the palm of her hand.

"I knew he'd have some," she declared.

She passed the warm coin to my husband. Looking down, he saw an old half-crown coin. Alf was dead, and half crowns had been out of circulation for many years!

Mrs Jenkins in her last year at Pwlldu.

Ma was never ill, I can't remember her ever even having a cold or a simple headache. Then in the winter of 1973, Miss Lily Jenkins received a message to say that she was quite ill and could not leave her bed. The Social Services were alerted and she was taken to Swansea Hospital. She made a partial recovery and was sent to Hill House to convalesce. When her Spartan living conditions in such a remote place were discovered, there was no question of her returning to Pwlldu. She was transferred to the old peoples' home at Glan-y-Mor, Penmaen. Grieving for her beloved Pwlldu, she even tried on two occasions to leave the Home and make her way back to the Valley, but she was discovered in Swansea, in a confused state. From this time she just faded away. She died in 1976, and part of Pwlldu died with her. The cottage, which had received no attention for years, became very dilapidated, the garden overgrown, and an air of utter desolation surrounded the place. There were no children, and apparently no members of the family wanted to live in the cottage. After at least 250 years, there were no members of the Jenkins family at Pwlldu.

Wrecks and Wrecking

WRECKS

Pwlldu Bay, has no strong currents within the Bay itself; the Needles provide natural shelter; indeed it is considered one of the safest bays on the Gower coast. But when storm conditions exist; with the accompanying violent wind, huge seas and poor visibility, the rocks of Pwlldu and the adjacent cliffs can be as savage as any other part of the coast, as many ships have discovered to their cost.

Many of the wrecks have gone unrecorded, the boats being too small and relatively unimportant. This, of course, is particularly true of wrecks pre-1900, when even human life was held cheap, and unless the cargo carried was particularly interesting and/or valuable, the only evidence of the disaster would be the wreckage washed up on the shore. As we have seen this was the fate of the many stone carrying 'muffies', wrecked in the 18th and 19th centuries. Similarly over the years, many small fishing vessels and ketches have come to grief either on the Needles rocks themselves or have been washed onto the sharp ledges of Hunt's Bay. There may have been a brief report of such wrecks in the local press, especially if loss of life was incurred. Two such reports were of the iron German ship the *Lammershagan*, which ran onto rocks below Pwlldu Head in 1882 and went to pieces; on this occasion the crew were saved and housed for a short time in Beaufort. The same year a schooner went ashore at almost the identical place; sadly in this instance the Captain drowned.

In Pwlldu's long history there are, however, two wrecks that were not only newsworthy at the time of the disaster, but their stories have been passed down the centuries and become part of the story of Pwlldu. In one instance, not only did the tale of the wreck survive but the name of the ship and the fate of its victims were recorded for all time on our Ordnance Survey maps of the area.

A glance at a large scale Ordnance Survey Map of the Gower coast will reveal two names: Caesar's Hole and Gravesend below Pwlldu Head.

The Wrecking of the 'Caesar'

As a child, growing up in Pwlldu, one of our many games had been 'hiding from the press-men'. Alf Jenkins had told us stories of how the men of the district, when they knew that a press-gang was in the area trying to locate local men to serve in His Majesty's fleet, would often take to the fields and hide until the danger was past. In the fields behind Webbs' Cottage, which at this time were part of Hunt's farm, there were about four quite deep pits. It is rumoured that one of them marks the ruins of an old chapel. In these depressions, men could crouch down and be hidden from immediate view. Arthur Jones told me that his great grandparents had passed down the story of how the children of the area, would go out into the fields with baskets, pretending to pick flowers or mushrooms; at the bottom of the baskets would be food for the hidden men. This story could well be true, as from early times, the press-gangs could arrest any man who did not have a protection certificate. The agricultural labourers and quarry men of Pwlldu would not have such papers and knew only too well that, if seized they would be forcibly removed and taken to Swansea where they would be secured safely below deck of a vessel; that would then take them to a port such as Bristol, Greenwich or Plymouth, where they were usually transferred to another ship that was bound for War. Sometimes they would be secured with ropes and the hatches slammed down on them; on other occasions they might have their hands actually manacled to the beams of the ship. This barbaric practice of manning the Navy by force was defended by the Government of the day, as the only practical way to secure sufficient recruits to defend our country against its enemies.

One of the many stories told to us at bedtime, usually in front of a roaring log fire, was the account of how the *Caesar* was wrecked. This tale held particular interest to us, as our cottage, that is Cliff Cottage where we were then living, actually featured in the story. I was told how one night in 1760, when a fearful storm was blowing outside and the occupants of the cottage were huddled around the fire, there came a loud knocking on the door. By the light of the lantern, which was always kept in its own niche in the wall of the porch, there was revealed the faces of two desperate looking men, their clothes soaking wet and dishevelled, asking if they were anywhere near Swansea. Alarmed at the men's appearance, they were refused entry to the cottage and sent on their way with instructions to take the path over the cliffs, which would eventually lead them to the town. With foul language, accompanied by many threats, they seized the lantern and disappeared into the unholy night.

It was many years later, when in college, that I first came across C. D. Morgan's *Guide to Gower*, written in 1860. In the book he gives a graphic description of how a press gang from a ship named the *Caesar*, had attempted to take a number of men on the sands near Swansea. The men, including a Mr John Voss of Nicholaston Hall, and his neighbour John Smith, put up a tremendous fight and eventually, with the help of Voss's brother and some other men, succeeded in overpowering the ship's officers who quickly made their escape.

This description seemed to authenticate many of the details that had come down through the centuries from the older generation, such as my grand-father.

These accounts tell of how the *Caesar* was finally firmly lodged into the rocks at the place now named 'Caesar's Hole'. Among the survivors were the Master and the Mate, the two men had obviously been able to somehow scramble over the bowsprit and make their way ashore. They had stumbled through the darkness, wind and rain, up the cliff, taking care not to plunge into the quarry which would have been immediately to their right. Following the edge of the cliff, the first dwelling they would have come to, would have been High

The path from Caesar's Hole over to High Pennard House (later known as Cliff Cottage). The gravestones can be detected at upper right.

Pennard House (Cliff Cottage). All they were concerned with was their own safety; not a word was said of the unfortunate men trapped in the hull of the broken ship, with the sea rising and before long trapping them into a watery grave.

It was not until next morning that news of the wreck swept through Pwlldu, High Pennard and probably as far as Bishopston and Pennard. Morbidly curious and hoping for rich pickings from the wreck, the country people made their way over the cliffs and down to the doomed ship. When the full horror of the situation was assessed, they would have felt no compunction in pilfering as many of the removable objects from the wreck as possible.

The bodies of the drowned men were also taken from the ship, and carried along the edge of the cliff, away from the greedy tide. Although the local people would have no doubt taken advantage of the wreck to procure any objects for their own use, they were not without compassion for the dreadful fate that had befallen the pressed men; after all it could so easily have been men from their own families that could have shared their fate.

It has been told how the villagers took the bodies to the nearest gully in the cliffs, where the soil had some depth and burial was possible. Not content with just burying the bodies, they marked the communal grave with an almost perfect circle of limestone rocks, which remains to this day. In Summer when the ferns are high, unless one knows exactly where to look, they are difficult to find. Sometimes when one of the frequent furze fires burn away the undergrowth, they are revealed quite starkly, the white limestone gleaming against the blackened furze. However, in Winter and Spring, they can still be located. Perhaps it is my imagination, but this spot has an atmosphere all of its own. Tourists very rarely visit it; even if they know of the grave's existence, they find it difficult to locate, and are not willing to take the rather steep long climb from the Needles rocks and then drop down into the very lovely valley. Many times I have sat on the gravestones and relived the events of this grisly tale, of 'man's inhumanity to man'. Yet there are redeeming features to the story. Mr Arthur Jones told me how his great grandmother was one of the local children who regularly visited the grave and put spring flowers on the stones, and were told by their parents not to forget 'the brave men' who lay buried there. Dr W. N. Jenkins has carried out some detailed research on the whole event and given some intriguing possible explanations as to how the ship came to be wrecked. His article appears in the *Gower Journal*, Vol. XXVI. It is very satisfactory to find how most of the details of the oral history tie in and complement the official records he has found. Of course the Admiralty neglects to mention the horrific drowning of the pressed men. It was left to the local people to record this event; it is their oral memory which has led to the naming of the now well-known Caesar's Hole, and the grave's location as 'Gravesend'.

S.S. Tours

I first came across the name of this vessel while researching the history of the Beaufort pub. From an entry in the Quarter Sessions I found that on June 8th, 1920, a successful prosecu-

S.S. Tours lying stranded on the rocks of Hunts, 1919.

tion had been brought against the former landlord for serving drinks after official hours. Several of the men who had been found drinking were members of the crew of the *S.S Tours*. So its wrecking on the rocks of Deepslade Bay (another name for Hunt's Bay) in October 1918 is very much part of the Pwlldu story.

It was to lie on the rocks for almost eight months. Then on the morning of Sunday, 29th June, 1919, efforts to refloat it were started. Once again the bush telegraph of the community went into high gear and before long every man, woman and child had heard of the refloating attempt. There may have been some secret hopes of some successful wrecking but most people just wanted to be witnesses to this very exciting and newsworthy event. Two such people were David and Ivor Jones who were there as small boys, and can still remember the event as if it had happened yesterday.

> *"You had to see it to believe it – it looked as if it had just been dropped there – it was standing as firm as a house – it might have been cemented into the rocks. We heard that it had come in on a huge tidal wave, so big that it had swept away a house at Caswell. The same wave had swept up the Bishopston Valley*

and demolished part of the bridge. Anyway me and my pal, Jack Beynon, who lived in a cottage in High Pennard, skipped school in order to see the boat. I remember telling him that there had been 40 men on board and they were all safe – back came the quick reply – 'You've got it wrong there were more men than that – at least 36!' . . . He was never very bright!

It lay on the rocks for eight months and we often went round to see it. Then we heard it was going to be refloated. Once more we sat on the cliffs – it was like a grandstand view. They brought down a big engine and then tried to blast away the rocks and cut a big track in the rocks so that she could slide down into the water. I remember they tried twice to get her off but she held fast. Then they brought round three tugs and they came round from Pwlldu Head. By now there were hundreds of people sitting on the grassy slopes and on the cliff top. See – they'd cut this ridge and then propped her up with great baulks of wood to stop her going over. Anyway they now started blasting away the timber. Then she started to move, and everyone cheered. We stood up we were so excited. She slid down the ridge which the men had greased, but suddenly she seemed to go on her side and lean out – we thought she was going to topple right over. Everyone groaned, you could hear it all over the cliff. Then as she hit the water, almost by magic, she righted herself and a gasp of relief went all around. The tide had come up by now and they attached her by ropes to the tugs. They somehow managed to pull her bows round – see, she was facing out to sea now! Then we noticed a flag appear on her mizzen mast and this must have been a signal for the tugs to start pulling. As she slid into the water, everyone gave a great cheer. I'll never forget that day!"

The ship was finally taken into Swansea for dry-dock repairs, so there was little chance for the locals to do any wrecking, but I am told by Mrs Connie Richards of Pennard that some of the timber used in the rescue operation was taken up the cliff and used in the building of the house called 'Channel View' which is still on the edge of the cliff road on the way to Southgate.

WRECKING

This romantic word in early history had very sinister implications. Without doubt in earlier years, it was not uncommon for villagers to lure ships onto the rocks, perhaps by placing lights strategically. The wrecked ships would then be looted and the 'prog' quickly removed to safe hiding places.

There is certainly no hint in the Pwlldu history to suggest that this happened on this part of the Gower coast, but wrecks have always played a part in community life. In the 18th and 19th century a wreck could be quite a bonus. By the time the customs were notified and had come from Swansea, the wreck would have been stripped and the cargo spirited away. The word 'wrecking' has remained in the Gower dialect and certainly all the inhabitants of the Valley and the cliffs use it even to this day.

To go wrecking means to search the shore line for literally anything that can be eaten, drunk, sold or used. Of course if the haul is of any value then the Excise Men, or later the coastguards should be informed. This rarely happened! There is an unwritten law that as far as wrecking is concerned, 'finding is keeping', and over the centuries this had led to many disputes, some of them quite unpleasant!

One such dispute occurred in the Jenkins family. A Chinese boat loaded with pit props was torpedoed off the Gower coast; before long every bay and inlet was awash with timber, as one local said, *"they came in like matchsticks"*. Pwlldu Bay was soon covered with this valuable cargo. Anxious to secure the logs before they could be swept out to sea and someone in Lynmouth or Porlock would benefit, Alf and Marion Jenkins of Pwlldu, together with Hezekiah Jenkins of Bishopston, spent many hours collecting the logs and bringing them safely above the tide line.

By this time the Excise Men had got wind of the haul, and made their way down the cliff. They cast a cursory glance over the pile of logs and when asked how many there were, were told that about 200 props had been taken from the shore. This figure was accepted by the Excise Men when in fact the true number was more like 300, and a charge of 1d per prop was made; each family paying for half the load. In the meantime Hezekiah Jenkins had arranged for a farm cart to take his 100 props up the steep cliff path to Bishopston. His task completed he returned to the beach, fully expecting to share out the remaining booty with Alf and Marion Jenkins.

Pwlldu Bay was deserted and there was no sign of any more pit props. The Jenkins of Pwlldu had won the game and while left on their own, had quickly spirited away the remaining props and safely stored them in their back garden. When challenged by Hezekiah, Marion Jenkins calmly replied that they each had 100 logs, half of the original load, as arranged with the Excise Officers. This was a perfect example of Gower cunning!

Right up until the 1970's, when the Jenkins left Pwlldu for good, all their fuel came from wrecked pieces of timber. As we know Ma Jenkins developed a very special skill in dealing with it.

Some of the best wrecking was in the First World War when many cargoes from destroyed ships would end up on the beach. Eddie Butcher remembers a day in 1918 when he awoke one morning to find the sea all orange; a mass of oranges had been swept ashore from a ship named the *Francis and Ann*. The very next day the sea had turned yellow, this time with a crop of lemons. The small boy collected buckets of the fruit but was later disappointed to find the oranges and lemons full of salt water and completely inedible.

Alf Jenkins remembered a timber ship being wrecked which had been loaded with floor joists (seven by two's). The whole of the Gower Coast was covered with them. Every cove was packed as they kept being driven ashore. The coastguards could not possibly keep a check on the whole cargo. Pwlldu beach was soon cleared and within hours not a plank was to be seen. I am reliably told that floors in Beaufort and Ship were repaired, and before long a few new wooden garden sheds and poultry houses appeared in the gardens. No doubt any surplus to requirements was sold or bartered for other goods. A close examination of the roof timbers in Beaufort will reveal quarter inch holes, that could only have been made by a marine borer, so when the inn was first built in the 1830's it would seem that 'wrecked' timber was used.

On one occasion a huge cask was washed up. Alf Jenkins immediately set out to examine it. First he kicked it, but there was no sound, so he knew that whatever was in the cask was probably solid. On opening the top of the barrel, he discovered it was full of bees wax! Ever the entrepreneur, he melted down the wax and using Ma's pudding basins, made it up into half pound pats. These he sold in the locality (Mrs Connie Richards of Pennard remembers buying one). He also took some into Swansea Market. All Alf's ladders were made from masts that had been washed in. In exactly the same way even today the Malt House is full of wonderful timber that has been washed ashore at some time. Indeed most of the many alterations to the house: windows, indoor furniture, bookshelves – all have been made from 'wreckage'. When my grand-daughter was very young she firmly believed that any special order given by her grand-father for a specific piece of wood, would be magically supplied by 'Davy Jones'. Hand-in-hand they would go down to the beach for some 'wrecking' and indeed sometimes the required length of wood would miraculously appear, and be quickly put to use.

A story is told of large barrels of spirits being washed ashore at Hunt's Bay. The Jones' of Hunt's quickly hid them in stacks of hay which stood in the fields after harvest. Excise Men were soon on the scene and obviously knew what they were looking for. They entered the field and fired guns into the stacks of hay. The precious liquid sprayed out and quickly soaked away into the ground. The farmers watched helplessly.

Even today wrecking continues to be one of my favourite pastimes. You never know what you're going to find. Over the years some amazing articles have been left on the tideline: rope, a ship's fender, plastic trays, plastic crates, buckets and jugs, beach balls, bathing costumes and towels, assorted beach shoes (never a pair) – in fact you name it and we've probably found it! One time a wonderful haul of bamboo fishing creels were washed in, probably from the River Severn; we didn't have to buy any bamboo supports for the garden for many years. Indeed I did wonder if the old bamboo summer house built in Beaufort garden by 'Grampy' in the 1930's might have come from a similar source.

Two World Wars

1914 – and in Lord Grey's sad words, *"the lights were going out all over Europe"*. The Kaiser had broken the treaty guaranteeing Belgian neutrality; his army swept towards Paris. Britain honoured her alliance with France and declared war. Optimists everywhere expected it to be over within a few months, but in less time than that, it had become bad.

A poignant reminder of this is a post-card of the bridge at Pwlldu sent to one of the very few young men from the Pwlldu area to be called to the Front. Young Minnie Lewis, who lived by the chapel in Murton and whose father used to farm some of the fields at Knapp, was writing to her brother at the front; she was convinced that by Christmas, the war would be over. From the whole Pwlldu, High Pennard and Bishopston area, only eight men lost their lives in the Great War; this, of course, was because almost all of the men were in reserved occupations.

Bridge at Pwlldu, 1914. (Minnie Lewis' postcard).

The demand for more and more food to be grown went out to every farmer. Meanwhile, German submarines were sinking ships laden with imported food on which this country had come to depend. Many cargoes were washed onto the beaches and claimed as wreckage.

Horses, even the cart-horses essential for farm work had been requisitioned and sent to the Front. Because of their isolation this does not seem to have happened in Pwlldu and High Pennard. However, orders came for more and more land to be ploughed, some of it land that had never been farmed before. Short of manpower, many farmers' sons left school early to help on the land.

Then, after four terrible years it all ended. The German army yielded, the Kaiser abdicated and the armistice was signed. Peace, so longed for, soon brought other troubles. But in the same way that the war itself had had so little impact on Bishopston, High Pennard and the Valley, the troubles that beset much of the rest of the country, and indeed the industrial areas of Swansea, were just not present. Imports of meat and corn meant that much of the arable land returned to pasture; this also meant that not so much labour was required. Some of the part-time agricultural labourers who had worked on the bigger farms were laid off and left the area to find work in Swansea. But as most of the farms were worked by single families, they continued much as they had always done, and there was little change in the pattern of life. There had always been a lack of money, so this was nothing new. There was still no piped water, no electricity and not enough skilled labour. On the farms and in the cottages there was no room for extravagance, but time and energy could take the place of money. This area was still a community where everyone helped everyone else, and troubles were shared. People still walked long distances and these people enjoyed their ham and eggs, or an occasional drink at a convivial bar. However, there is no doubt that the takings at Beaufort were slightly down; this could well have been in part due to the rise of the Temperance Movement and the Band of Hope. All the Jones boys at their mother's insistence had taken the pledge when they were quite young. The older men still enjoyed their drink but many of the younger men were becoming tee-totallers.

I Enter the Pwlldu Story

My grand-father, Mr Ivor L. Roberts, a well-known Swansea garage proprietor, had rented Cliff Cottage, High Pennard, from Mrs Gilbertson in 1938. My uncle, Ivor Roberts, together with four friends, had often camped in a huge bell tent in one of Alice Jones' fields, behind High Pennard Farm. On one such holiday they happened to hear that Cliff Cottage was available to rent. The rest of the family all loved Pwlldu and knew the area well. My grandfather took little persuasion to take on the tenancy of the cottage. One of my earliest memories of Pwlldu is when Mrs Gilbertson called on my grandfather to collect the rent. The gracious old lady would always consent to stay for a cup of tea. The best china was put out, together with a plate of Nana's famous Welsh-cakes. After a short exchange of local news, my grandfather would place the rent on the round marble topped table (which is now in the garden at Beaufort), hands would be shaken, and that was that! – no papers to sign, no accounts taken, this was a gentleman's (and gentle lady's!) agreement that was honoured on both sides until Mrs Gilbertson's death.

Cliff Cottage had not changed for at least two hundred years and this was part of its charm. However our family continued to grow and before long there were four children and six adults all using the cottage on a regular basis; accommodation was stretched to the limit; something had to be done. My father and uncle decided to adapt the old cowsheds adjoining the cottage, into further living quarters. A new floor and roof were put in, together with a partition down the centre, so providing us with two reasonably sized rooms; one for each young family. A year or two later my uncle's family placed a caravan in the quite large garden, so that in effect we now had three self contained living areas.

So began my life-long association with this magical place. Looking back at my early years in Pwlldu, I remember what

Cliff Cottage in 1949, with the author sitting in the window.

fun we had, and what freedom. The whole area was one vast playground – the quarry, the beach, the Valley, the cliffs – all provided a life endlessly absorbing and varied. Is this nostalgia for a distant high spirited youth? I think it is more than that. As it was to young Eddie Butcher before me, Pwlldu for me was a wild and wonderful place, even its remoteness was part of its charm, and the simple pleasures it offered made my life richly satisfying then, and have had an enduring influence on the rest of my life. True, except for the war years I could only sample it at week-ends and holidays, but over the years our family became part of the community and in our own small way I like to think we were able to become good neighbours to the people around us.

The Second World War

To my parents the Second World War came as no surprise. Once war was declared, ruthless war from the air was expected and the English Channel would no longer form a line of defence. Orders were given and enforced at once that all windows were to be darkened completely. I can remember mother making 'black-outs', not only for our Swansea home, but also for Cliff Cottage. My mother had a heart complaint and so was entitled to a small petrol allowance which did enable us to still make occasional visits to Cliff Cottage. We had never even bothered with curtains in the countryside, nobody worried who looked into the windows, but now we had to remember German planes overhead, and even our torches had to have pieces of paper inserted to dim the light of the bulb.

Before long my father joined the Royal Air Force and my mother, a semi-invalid, was left with a child of nine and a young toddler of three to look after, with no help, other than occasional visits from my aunt, uncle and grandparents.

Then the bombs started to fall on Swansea. In our house in the Uplands, a Morrison shelter had been built in the middle room downstairs, and every night this is where we were put to bed. My father urged my Mother to move the family to High Pennard, where my aunt and cousins were already living. At first she refused, thinking no doubt of the lack of any basic facilities such as water and electricity, and the hard life she would face bringing up two young children, one of whom was little more than a baby, in such a remote place under such Spartan conditions.

She was soon to change her mind. In February, 1941 we experienced the first night of the three nights blitz on Swansea; it was a night that would never leave my memory. At the time I was suffering from pneumonia. Already running a high temperature and slightly delirious, I could still sense the utter terror of my Mother, as she listened for the tell-tale whine of a bomb falling somewhere near. Before the explosion could take place, cushions were hastily placed over our faces, to help shield us from any flying glass or other debris. The whole night even now remains a nightmare.

Next morning, with a toddler and a very sick child, my mother loaded the car with as many provisions, blankets, clothes and other essentials she could think of. There was a thin layer of snow on the ground. Bundled to the eyes in blankets, I remember staring out of the windows, as we started our journey. There had been several direct hits on our road during the night and we passed piles of still smoking rubble where once houses had stood.

The drive across the cliffs from Southgate to High Pennard was only just possible. The road was still little more than a grass track, with cart ruts at the side. The large pot-holes every few yards were filled with snow and quite invisible until we hit them with a sickening crunch. Slowly my mother inched her way along. At the top of the small rise that leads down to Cliff Cottage she stopped and changed into bottom gear; she dare not apply the brakes. Later I learnt she had said a small prayer as the car slithered and slid down to its destination, finally coming to rest on the mercifully flat ground outside the pig-sty. *"Well, we made it,"* she said, and promptly burst into tears. At nine years of age I was old enough to appreciate her terror and overwhelming relief; I joined in her tears.

From the bedroom windows of the cottage I had a grand-stand view of what was happening in Swansea. The next two nights I watched, enthralled at what I only thought of as a gigantic fireworks display. Bombs exploded in circles of light; long beams from the searchlights criss-crossed as they stab-bed across the sky, trying to trap an enemy bomber. Fires could often be seen on the skyline; we could hear the throb of the engines of the German bombers as they came in from the sea and droned up the valley. Even the incessant whine of bombs falling, added to the excitement. Incredibly, there was no sense of fear. I knew that Swansea was suffering another terrible night of destruction, but somehow it was far away, nothing to do with me. I was safe in my beloved Pwlldu. Germans couldn't reach me here.

So began two of the most exciting and interesting years of my life. To live in Pwlldu all the year round was nothing short of sheer bliss. I am almost ashamed to admit that, apart from the absence of my father, and the death of my dear Uncle Ivor who lost his life at Singapore, the horrors of the Second World War passed me by. In Pwlldu, there were no papers, no television, only a small battery wireless set which was used by my 'Pops' and Uncle Arthur to listen to the news. My grandparents were also now living at the cottage and from snatches of adult conversation that I overheard I realised that indeed there was a horrid war going on, but somewhere else, far away from where we were living; the fear and dread that the bombing in Swansea had produced, was never to return.

Although not called up, those men left at home were expected to help in any way they could.

In 1940, the new National Government's appeal for Local Defence Volunteers had even reached Pwlldu; as David Jones said, *"we were all supposed to be in something."*

He, together with some of his mates in Bishopston, joined the local battalion of the Home Guards. His sergeant was a veteran from the 1914-18 war. There were a few parades but little else; as he says, *"I didn't clean my gun once – I was excused a lot!"*

In fact the men became so bored that they decided to throw a dinner party for the battalion which was to be held in the old Swan Bus Garage in Bishopston. Charlie Musgrove, who was also a farmer, was to supply the meat, David Jones the potatoes and vegetables, while Charles Macnamara, who was known to be a handy man around the house, was prevailed upon to do the cooking. The meal was not a success! The meat was tough, the vegetables undercooked, and the whole event a disaster; although it did provide a talking point for years to come!

Few bombs fell in the area throughout the war, but there were still Air Raid Wardens who like the Home Guards had to pretend to be doing something. David Jones' next door neighbour was one such man. When the first siren went, he quickly came out of his house, immaculately dressed in his spanking new uniform, complete with tin hat. He stood in the front garden, quite at a loss as to what he was expected to do! He turned to his wife who had followed him out and asked her

The lone telegraph pole marking the position of Pwlldu Coastguard Station (World War II).

if she had any ideas. *"Blow your whistle, George. Blow your whistle."*

As the strident notes of the whistle shattered the silence, all the neighbours came out to see what had happened. Some were convinced the Germans had landed!

If one glances up the cliff on the right hand side of the beach, on a grassy incline, there still stands a lone telegraph pole. This is all that remains of the coastguard hut that was situated here from the beginning of the war. Here another group of local men were employed to keep a constant watch on the Bristol Channel for the presence of enemy vessels. We children were very excited when men from the post office came to set up a telegraph line all the way down the cliff to the hut – a telephone in Pwlldu Bay was something very new! The men were supposed to chart and be able to recognise all the different ships that were in the Channel, but as Harry Phillips confessed, *"I didn't know one boat from another. The only boats we could recognise was a rowing boat or a yacht!"*

His fellow Coastguards of Pwlldu were no more confident. Ernie Tucker from Pennard and Alfred Watkins from Hunt's

Farm usually did a shift together, and often on the way home, after a particularly boring day, they would call at Knapp Farm to see their old friend, Ivor Jones, and have a cup of tea. Ivor well remembers one such occasion when he asked them teasingly, *"What would you do, Ernie, if the Germans did come in here?"*

The reply came quickly and positively – *"I'd run like hell!"*

The Pwlldu and Pennard stations were manned by six men, four of whom were called 'regulars ' who were expected to work shifts around the clock, two men would take a shift of four to five hours. The other two men, who were part-time coastguards, would take the night shifts: 8 p.m.–1 a.m. and 1 a.m.–6 a.m. Harry Phillips worked part-time and hated getting up in the early hours of the morning. However there were compensations – he was paid £3-4 shillings a week – and even more important, he met his future wife while he was on duty!

At this time there was a path down the cliff from Cliff Cottage directly to the Coastguard hut, known as the 'short cut'. Down this path we would scramble, and spend hours just watching the coastguards. Sometimes Alf and Hezekiah Jenkins, who were the other members of the Pwlldu group, would be on duty and occasionally Mr Jinks would talk to us about German submarines, and if he was in a particularly good mood, we were allowed a quick look through his field glasses. Gone were the games of smugglers and quarrymen – now we became soldiers guarding our precious bay from enemy invasion.

Where Moses Road passes in front of the ruins of Rachel's Cottage, the track becomes very narrow and there is a sharp drop from the cliff down to the river. This is where the road was mined. In the event of an invasion, the mines could be quickly detonated; any advance up the cliff to Bishopston and ultimately Swansea would be blocked. Anyway that was the plan! However the fuse that was necessary to detonate the mines was not left with Alf Jenkins, the local man, but given to some official in Caswell. As Ivor Jones said, *"fat lot of good that was – the Germans would have been up the cliff, long before he could be called!"*

One of the earliest bombing raids on Swansea was when two

landmines were dropped, one destroying Woolworth's stores, the other a direct hit on the lock gates of the docks. The plane carrying these bombs flew directly up the Valley from the sea. Ivor Jones, who at the time was living in Knapp Farm, remembers it well, *"It was so low, I felt I could touch it – it flew up through the Valley between us and Mrs Gilbertson's – I can hear the low drum of its engines even now as I think of it . Next morning we found pieces of shrapnel in the valley, close to the explosion."*

There were bombs, even in this area. A shell landed in the front room of Paradise Meadows; luckily Mrs Gilbertson and her daughter were in the adjoining room and though very shocked, were not seriously hurt. On another occasion a German plane returning home after a raid on Swansea, unloaded his bombs and they fell in an arc right across the top of the Pennard cliffs. The nearest explosion to Pwlldu Bay was from the bomb that fell at Hunt's. Luckily no-one was hurt and no great damage done.

As the danger of invasion lessened in the second year of the war, the need for more home-grown food increased. Germany controlled the entire southern coast of the English Channel, Ireland was neutral; the convoys of food ships and oil-tankers were in constant danger. So the War Agricultural Committees were appointed to intensify farm production. Orders came for more and more land to be ploughed, some of it land that had never been farmed before. In High Pennard, the land immediately in front of Cliff Cottage, known as 'The Pit', which previously had always remained a huge patch of fern and bracken, was now ploughed up and used to grow highly successful crops of potatoes and vegetables. Everybody with a bit of garden was encouraged to 'Dig for Victory'. We have already learnt how the gardens of Beaufort and the Jenkins responded to the call. In High Pennard every available cottage garden was dug up and planted with vegetables. Bob Hughes was well-known for the quality of his vegetables. His wife, Lily, would deliver them to all the local cottages and houses, right along the cliffs as far as Southgate. They also had their own stall in the market.

Webbs' Cottage was now known as Sunnyside, and was occupied by two middle-aged ladies, Miss Seal and Mrs Moore, who was a German. They employed a full-time gardener, whose name was Price. He had a wonderful vegetable garden and Mrs Moor used to take them in her beautiful little pony and trap right out to the car-park at Southgate where she would sell them to the visitors and the local people, giving all the proceeds to the Red Cross. This noble act did not prevent some local paranoia about her nationality and all sorts of rumours were circulating; some people were even convinced she signalled to German submarines from her garden which looked directly out to sea. I am ashamed to admit that we children were as bad as anyone else, and spent many hours trying to spy on her and catch her out in some suspicious act.

Short of manpower, many farmers' sons left school early to help on the land. As most of his casual labourers had been called up, David Jones, like many other farmers, had to rely on Contractors; a request would be made to the Government and the requisite work would be carried out, and then the Government would have to be paid. He was also glad to employ Prisoners of War. These were stationed in Scurlage. The farmers would indicate how much help they needed and the required number of prisoners would be duly dropped off from a van which took them around the farms. Lower Hareslade Farm always needed extra help to plant the potato crop, which was still done by hand, and on one such occasion a group of eight Italian prisoners under the direction of a sergeant were taken on to augment the labour force on the farm. They were duly directed to work in a field of about 5 acres, which directly skirted the Bay. On going down to see how the work was going, David Jones was astonished to find an empty field, with no sign of the prisoners, all work had apparently ceased. Looking around he saw the sergeant who rather shamefacedly said the men were just taking a break. The Italians were found sitting on the cliffside enjoying the view – As David Jones remarked *"There was never much work in Italians!"*

Picking potatoes was another back breaking job, and this is when land-girls came into their own. Unlike the prisoners, they are remembered as girls not afraid of hard work, who did everything asked of them willingly and with a sense of fun. Starting the day by 9 a.m., they would have picked two tons of potatoes by 4 p.m. The bagging of the potatoes was also done on the farm, with the help of Mrs David Jones. Sitting on the trailer, her husband would pass the sacks up to her, and she would have the task of tying a length of cord securely round the head of each sack. Two tons of bagged potatoes would then be sent to the wholesalers in Alexandra Road.

Everyone managed and was proud of it. After all this was what they had been doing for hundreds of years, the war made little difference. Again neighbourliness was a lifeline, and everyone helped everyone else.

My Mother was known to be 'poorly', so Lizzie Jones who lived in the next cottage up the cliff, came daily to help clean the cottage, and empty the earth privy, which was located in the old pig sty at the end of the cliff. She also helped with the washing; ironing was done with flat irons heated one after another on the fire. In the small outhouse built onto the side of the cottage stood the copper boiler, together with the washtub and the old cast iron mangle. The same copper would provide us with hot water for a luxurious bath in a tin tub which was placed in front of the fire. Our hair was washed with beautifully soft rain water drawn from the large wooden casks kept in front of the cottage. Later we would curl up in the wooden inglenook at the side of the wide fireplace, where the huge chimney rose in steps to the wide open view of the sky. I remember how on a stormy night, rain, hailstones or very occasionally, snowflakes, would fall onto the glowing logs with a wonderfully satisfying sizzling noise. This was the time to stare into the magical green and blue flames from the logs and listen to the thrilling tales of the past, often told by my grandfather.

Alice Jones, who farmed alone in High Pennard Farm, supplied us with milk, cream, butter and cheese. This was a farm I dreaded visiting – not because of Alice, who was a kind, motherly soul, but because in order to reach the farm, I had first of all to negotiate a path through a large gaggle of very ferocious geese. They would advance on me, their long necks protruding in front of them, their yellow beaks ready to take lumps out of my bare legs; and all the time making a continuous, menacing, hissing sound. There was no way back. I had to reach that back door which led directly into the Dairy. Plucking up all my courage, shouting as loud as I could, and brandishing a long stick, I would finally make it. Alice would usually have been alerted by the noise of the geese, and would be waiting to greet me, a knowing smile on her weather-beaten face. Inside, the dairy was cool and spotlessly clean. The long narrow lean-to building was built quite separately from the kitchen, but alongside it. Running right around both long walls was a low shelf built from large slates; the shelf rested on upright columns of brick. On these shelves stood the large shallow pans of clotted cream cooling. In other pans, milk would be waiting for the cream to rise to the top. I well remember how Alice would take a flat wooden skimmer and carefully skim over the surface of the milk to recover the cream. This would then be poured into a jam-jar ready for me to carry home. Sometimes, when my grand-mother was at the cottage, I would take back a jug of skimmed milk which was used by her to make the most mouth-watering Welsh-cakes. Milk for drinking, still warm from the cows, would be poured into a lidded green enamel can, kept especially for the purpose.

In front of the farm, among the unfriendly geese and the foraging chickens, were two friendly pigs who would always be ready for a soft word and a little back scratching.

I well remember these pigs being killed. My mother had expressly forbidden me to attend such a blood-thirsty scene; it was not a suitable sight for a small girl; so, of course, I was even more determined to witness this exciting event. The ghastly screaming of the pig as the knife made its first quick cut, still remains with me to this day. The pig was then hauled onto a wooden bench with its stiff legs protruding over the front. It was at this stage I couldn't quite face the blood pouring out into the large enamel bowls held by Alice Jones and her two helpers, Lily Hughes and Lizzie Jones. Their hands would whip the blood so that it had no time to coagulate. This would later be made into blackpot (a kind of black pudding).

A flurry of work would follow. The bacon was packed into big crock salters, the hams would be cured in another one, usually with weak beer, honey and salt petre, finally being hung on big meat hooks embedded in the wooden beams that were part of every cottage ceiling. Every other part of the pig was used; sausages and brawn etc. As we have seen the pig had always been an essential part of every homestead; now in wartime it was even more important.

As well as the products from the pig there was plenty of wild meat to be had by snaring, trapping or shooting. Rabbits abounded on the farms and cliffs, and were shot in their hundreds by the farm boys; even the odd pheasant, sometimes injured and left in a stray bush, would be bagged and taken triumphantly home. There were still plenty of crabs and lobsters in the rocks, and fish from the sea; my uncle became an excellent fisherman and crabber. My particular love was for wild mushrooms which grew in great quantity on the cliffs. You had to get up early to find the best ones. One of my most delightful memories is of stealing from my bed while the rest of the family were still asleep, making my way onto Pwlldu Head and following the path around the cliff towards Hunts. The feel of the springy turf still wet from the early morning dew, against my bare feet (I hardly ever wore shoes); the coconut scent from the gorse; the slightly chill, pure morning air before the sun was fully risen, and oh, the excitement, as I suddenly came across the pale, gleaming heads of the huge horse mushrooms nestling in the green grass. In Summer and Autumn, when the wild fruits and the nuts ripened, picking was a pleasure as well as providing fruit to a wartime diet that only occasionally included citrus fruit. Blackberry picking has always been one of my delights, especially from the low growing bushes that flourish on the stone pebbles that fringe the beach; the hot sun is reflected off the stones and often the fruit is ripened quite early in the season. The deep gullies formed from the old quarry workings down on the grits also provide rich picking grounds, the bushes are protected from the ravages of the weather and the sheltered slopes provide bushes with large succulent berries that are free from any pollution except the slight salty tang of the sea.

All our fresh vegetables came from Bob Hughes' Farm; indeed all our needs were supplied by our immediate neighbours; we wanted for nothing. Of course being the eldest child I was the one who had to go for all these provisions. On the whole I thoroughly enjoyed doing so; most of my neighbours loved a chat and even allowed me to help them in their tasks around the farm. I remember hay-making in the Hughes farm with Gwynfor Hughes who was the same age as me and who went to the same school. Most of this was still done by hand and our job was to rake the hay up and toss it onto the top of the growing stack placed on the horse drawn cart. The huge hay barn was a favourite play place, and many secrets were told and shared in the completely hidden dens at the top of the high stack.

At this time herds of sturdy Gower ponies could often be seen grazing at the Bay's edge. They were tamed at need for rough riding, but most of the year they wandered at will wherever they could find good pasture. Pwlldu was one of their favourite places. Even during the severest winter, they could be seen in droves, getting their scanty fare from the banks of the Bishopston stream. In the Spring, the new foals would be born, and this event provided me with an unforgettable experience. On

A one hour old foal is introduced to the rest of the wild herd.

the stones, just outside the Beaufort, I noticed that the herd had formed a circle, in the middle of which, something exciting seemed to be happening. I crept forward, making as little noise as possible, and positioned myself at a good vantage point. I quickly realised that I was about to witness the birth of a foal. In no time, a long slippery bundle of quivering flesh was delivered onto the clean, rounded pebbles. The Mother commenced licking away the birth sac and in no time at all, a tiny foal was standing on quivering, spindly legs, looking around the circle of horses that surrounded him. Then came the magic – one by one each pony from the herd approached the tiny foal and licked it; it had been accepted and welcomed into its new large family.

The war had even provided me with companions. Within the first few days of the war thousands of town children were dispatched to country billets, and four of these had been placed in Beaufort. To my delight they were all girls, and being the same age as me, quickly became friends. They were from London, spoke with strong cockney accents and had never seen the sea before in their whole lives! Shortly after their arrival the two James sisters had found them wading into the sea, fully dressed! They were not the only evacuees from London; three girls were billeted in Pennard. A wonderful story is told of an incident that is hilarious in the telling, but could have ended very tragically. Apparently while playing on the beach, the three girls came upon an unexploded mine. One of the girls tore up the cliff to tell of their find. She was quickly taken to the only house with a telephone, so that the coastguards could be alerted. Speaking into the telephone she calmly told the coastguards that there was no need to hurry, as her two sisters were sitting on the mine in order to 'mind it'!!!!

Clothing a family in wartime was a nightmare, as clothing coupons rarely allowed for new garments. In Pwlldu this did not seem to matter. Living the life we did, in the depths of the country, we did not need many 'best' clothes. Indeed apart from school, I wore a dress as seldom as possible, always shorts and tops, even in the Winter when the weather was cold or wet; at most I put on an old woolly jacket; somehow we didn't seem to feel the cold. Except in Winter when the weather was very cold, we always tried to go barefoot everywhere; indeed the soles of our feet became as hard as leather. Like young Eddie Butcher before me, my companions were often the farm boys, and we all hated shoes and only wore them to school or if we visited town. In the community as a whole, dress was unimportant, except for a few special occasions. In High Pennard, the women would rarely leave the cottages and farms, so often the same couple of dresses would be worn daily. I always remember Lizzy and Alice Jones, Lily Hughes and indeed Ma Jenkins always wearing aprons over their clothes. If they were working in the farmyards, the apron would sometimes be substituted by an old piece of sacking tied around the waist, and if it was raining, around the shoulders too. The men would be similarly protected, so their well worn corduroys would hopefully last that much longer. Best summer frocks would be kept for visits to town, church, or social occasions, such as harvest suppers, shows, or village fêtes.

One such village fête I well remember. It was held on Mrs Moore's lawn at Sunnyside. Price was given the task of erecting a huge maypole, and the two ladies managed to somehow get hold of yards of coloured ribbons which were duly fastened to the top. Mrs Moore gathered together some twenty children from all the neighbouring farms and cottages: the four evacuees from Beaufort; some girls from the bungalow field behind Cliff Cottage, boys from Hughes and Hunt's farms, altogether forming a motley crew, who had to be bullied, cajoled and threatened into performing a simple country dance while weaving the ribbons from the top of the pole to the bottom, then reversing the process until all the ribbons were safely unravelled. I can remember the great fun we had during rehearsals when the ribbons became so entangled that Price would have to come to the rescue and try to sort out the knot. In the meantime we would have bumped into our partners and collapsed in giggles on the floor. The farm boys thought the whole exercise 'sissy' and had to be bribed to stay. The day arrived, the weather was perfect (indeed all my memories of Pwlldu took place in perfect weather!); wonder of wonders, our dance was a success. A handsome sum was donated to the Red Cross.

Our wonderful free life continued. Even school was an adventure. The long journey across the cliffs to Southgate, through the village, and then down the Cwmbs to Parkmill. Together with Gwynfor Hughes from the farm I undertook this journey every day in all weathers, and thought nothing of it. The village school served the Parishes of Pennard and Parkmill and there were only two classes taught in one long room, divided by a glass partition. Mr Evans, the headmaster was a delightful man and adored by most of the pupils. I seemed to spend little time on the three 'R's', far preferring to learn the names of the wild flowers which we studied on our frequent walks in Ilston woods. Gwynfor Hughes' memory of the school is that after registration he was sent into the school garden where he would spend most of the day; he became known as the head gardener! Consequently when the dreaded scholarship exam finally arrived, it made little or no impact on us, and not surprisingly I failed.

This woeful event made my parents come to a momentous decision – we had to return to Swansea at once, so that I could be properly prepared for my 'over-age' exam, the last chance I had of getting a scholarship to the Grammar School. Our full-time occupation of Cliff Cottage was over.

Yesterday Ending

After the Second World War, change was in the air; new families had settled in the area; farms and estates were broken up and sold; even the landscape was altering. These changes did not happen all at once, and to the casual visitor they would not even have been obvious, but they were happening at an ever increasing pace; indeed it could be argued that 'yesterday' ended in the 1950's.

The Decline of Farming

The small farms in High Pennard had all but disappeared. Cliff Cottage, Webbs Cottage (now Kilsaran), had already become private homes. Bob Hughes and his eldest son had emigrated to Canada in 1948, and the farm was sold as a private house. Hunts and Lower Hareslade were still successful farms, but even here there were widespread changes in farming practice. Mechanisation was taking over the back-breaking grind of heavy manual labour. The passing of animal traction meant the gradual disappearance of the horses which had called for so much skill in handling. The farmer was becoming less of a husbandman, more like an agricultural mechanic, the rural counterpart of the factory machine-minder. David Jones recalls how in 1949 he was able to purchase tractors which during the war had been used to pull planes. These had been refurbished and for £360 the farmer had a reasonable second-hand tractor which lasted quite a long time. However, even with mechanisation, farming was still very hard work. In 1983, after a lot of heart searching, David and his wife decided to leave the farm. There were no sons to carry on, rents were continually climbing, and above all the couple wanted to be able to spend the last part of their lives, enjoying their leisure and having more time to spend with their children and grandchildren. So after more than two hundred years the Jones family stopped farming. Lower Hareslade which the family had farmed for a hundred years, was sold; the house became a private residence, and the land sold off in two lots of 27 acres.

It is interesting that this land, together with six fields previously farmed at the Knapp, was bought by a retired schoolteacher. He even got planning permission to build a farmhouse; the land was used as pasture for sheep and for the rearing of cattle.

By the 1970's a general countrywide decline in farming took place, setting the trend for the part-time farmer. The other Jones family, with an equally long history of farming, on the well-known Great Kittle Farm, was also to disappear from the farming scene. The house, together with five acres of land, has just been sold as a private residence. The land has been sold off to cattle dealers, and to riding stables to provide grass for their ponies.

The same fate has befallen the fields along Pwlldu Lane for so long farmed by Mr David Jones (Sen) and his sons. Today they have been sold off separately by a dealer to local riding stables.

The Knapp, which has featured so largely in the Pwlldu story, is no longer a farm. This charming farmhouse perched on the top of the cliff on the Bishopston side of the Bay, has also become a private home. When Ivor Jones finished farming there in 1958, it was bought by Mrs Lechmere Oertel, a niece of Mr Frank Gilbertson. The land has been sold off in small lots; indeed some of it is still for sale.

Ivor Jones moved to High Pennard Farm and continued to farm until the 1970's. When he retired, the farm was bought by his son, Alan Jones, who still did some farming, but was also employed by British Petroleum. His brother still farms some of the fields, including some land that used to be farmed by Bob Hughes; he runs a pig farm, but is also employed in another capacity.

View up the Valley from the bridge – wild but still beautiful.

Changes in the Landscape

Gower landscape owes its essential character to the continuance of traditional farming; with the decline of the farming community in Pwlldu and its environs, there was bound to be an effect on the landscape. No longer could sheep be seen grazing on broad open water meadows, skirting the Bay and Valley. Gradually from the 1950's on, Nature took over the woods and fields which had once been so carefully maintained. The banks of the stream flowing into the Bay have all but disappeared, being covered with dense undergrowth and hawthorn, ash and sloes that have seeded themselves, not always in the best places. The reeds have grown thickly and access to the stream is almost impossible; it would be futile to even attempt to find the lovely natural spring that came from the bank above the bridge and supplied both houses in the valley with drinking water. No longer can children play on grassy slopes bordering the stream, while even if the old dipping stone could be found, access to it would be impossible.

Even the clifflands are different in character. The farmers used to depend on the young green furze both for feed and bedding, so twice a year, in early Spring and late Autumn, a carefully controlled fire of the furze took place in order to encourage new growth. It was not only young fern that was encouraged to grow but a myriad of wild flowers would stud the ground among the new growth. It can be argued that this untamed Nature provides equally enchanting pictures: the wind rippling through the reed beds; a moorhen and her babies enjoying the secrecy of the reeds as they swim in an arc down the stream; badgers making their sets by the fallen tree trunks that lie haphazardly over the water; the bird population has certainly made use of the variety of habitat and it is doubtful whether there is anywhere in Gower that can offer so many different species.

The beach remains the same; the tall Needles rocks with the three cormorants that are always to be seen sitting on the top of the ring rock; the wide sandy beach fringed with its locally unique bank of rounded pebbles.

Access to the bay is still very difficult. At the end of the 1950's the road from Hunts to Pwlldu was surfaced with tarmacadam, most of the work being done by the Jones family. Mr Hopkins of Sandy Lane, who was in the trade, did manage to provide the tarmac at a special price, and deliver it for them, even so it cost £3000. The people who owned properties adjoining the road shared the cost. However this remains a private road and can only be used by residents, and no parking is allowed along the cliff top. The steep, stony path to the beach is in a worse condition than ever before. Running rain water has eroded the surface and the red ash laid down by the Council has all been washed away. The steps that were built at the same time have become very dangerous. Now only rarely used by residents and a few hardy tourists, brambles and furze are quickly taking over the path. It is hard to believe that at one time, not that long ago, this was the main road to Swansea for the crofters and farmers of High Pennard.

On the Bishopston side of the Bay the local City Council and the Bishopston Community Council have wisely decided

Steep rock path to High Pennard, now too rough even for slide cars.

that Pwlldu must remain a 'Walkers Bay'. Both bodies have recognised the dangers from badly parked cars and vehicles trying to reverse down the lane when they find the small car park at the end of Pwlldu Lane is full. After careful consideration it has been decided to close the car park. Moses Road which leads down to the bay is still very dangerous for any vehicle that does not have a four wheel drive. It is just negotiable for the Pwlldu residents, who have vehicular right of way. The only other legal users of the road are the emergency services such as fire, police and Marine Rescue; also the National Trust and the City Countryside officials, all of whom are often called out in a busy summer season. Some people may complain about the state of these roads, but without any doubt, the difficult access has helped to make sure that the bay has been able to retain its special character.

Its protection was further enforced when Gower was made an Area of Outstanding Beauty; then in 1954, Mrs Gilbertson and her daughter Mrs Hugh Vivian, gave the whole of the Bishopston Valley to the National Trust. These two measures together with continued vigilance from the Gower Society have prevented any form of commercialisation.

The National Trust has also done some sterling work in the Valley which is still recognised as possibly the most beautiful in Gower. The impervious shale floor does not easily absorb rainwater and so is often flooded. With the help of volunteers the Trust has looped the old path onto higher ground so that the flooded area can be avoided; a wooden footbridge has also been constructed over the ground where the stream has invaded the old path. Some would argue that these improvements have not added to the natural unspoilt nature of the Valley, but they have enabled many people to walk its length without being completely immersed in mud.

Among the increasing number of regular visitors are the happy bands of city children who stay in Kilvrough Manor at all times of the year, and, dressed in their distinctive bright orange anoraks, walk down the Valley to the beach. In our family they have affectionately been christened 'the Ladybirds'.

The population of Bishopston has increased continuously and rapidly during this century. The beginning of the growth was due to its position as an important supplier of agricultural products for Swansea Market, but as transport improved, its potential as a commuting centre for Swansea was developed. The land that was once used for 22 market gardens was now taken over for housing estates. The same population increase was experienced in Pennard, but happened rather later. During the decade 1961-1971, its rate of growth was the highest in the Gower Peninsula. Of course these new residents have become frequent visitors to Pwlldu, especially those living in Bishopston, who quite rightly have a certain protective attitude towards their own local beach, and are determined to guard its fragile beauty.

New People in the Valley

The cottages in High Pennard which had for a hundred years or more housed farm labourers and quarry worker, have now become homes for people drawn from many walks of life. Some cottages are occupied all the year round by people who love the remoteness of the area and are quite prepared to put up with some of the inconveniences, just to have the privilege of living in a corner of Gower which is still largely unspoilt. Others have become second homes for people who have discovered the scenic beauty of this tucked away part of Gower, and visit it on a regular basis, sometimes for many years, so even they become part of the community.

The two old inns on the beach, for so long the hub of the community, have changed hands many times over the years. Seduced by the beauty of their setting, many families have attempted to live there all the year round, only to be beaten by the stresses and strains of modern life. The remoteness of the location, with its attendant difficulties of access, finally forced them to leave. Until the advent of the four wheel drive vehicle, the only access to the Valley was to walk up the steep stony cliff to the end of Pwlldu Lane where a car could have been parked. Husbands going to work accompanied by children who had to be in school on time, found this daily walk in all weathers, an unbearable burden. Finally both houses are occupied by retired couples who do not have any regular time restrictions in their lives, and have the leisure time to fully enjoy their lovely environment, and maintain the labour intensive large gardens.

There are new people in the two big houses at the head of the Valley, previously occupied by members of the Gilbertson and Vivian family. In the late 1960's, for a short time Paradise Meadow even became a hotel.

The Community

The wonderful community spirit that has always been such a feature of this area, is still there even though it has changed in character. No longer do the same families live in the same houses for generations. Perhaps the one element that draws the community together now is the peoples' genuine and abiding love for Pwlldu and the life it provides. No longer linked by marriage, residents do still know each other and are delighted to help out in any emergency. We may not work together to harvest hay or wash sheep; but when a Land Rover gets stuck

Neighbourly help.

in a flooded river, or a vehicle gets blocked on the cliff track, it is still the neighbours who come to the rescue. There may be no more harvest suppers or threshing dinners, but Beaufort and Ship still enjoyed a joint street party to celebrate the Royal Wedding. Both houses often join together for midnight swims and summer barbecues. When children grow up, they invariably move away and marry people outside the Pwlldu area; their partners could be from other parts of Wales, England or indeed the rest of the world! But if they have had any form of close contact with Pwlldu, either from living there at some time in their lives, or even as a frequent holiday visitor, they always return, usually bringing their own young children with them. My children, while students at college, would return on many week-ends, bringing with them fellow students who would marvel at the remote beauty of the area. Now married and living away from home, they bring their children as often as they can. In Beaufort and Ship the many grandchildren who visit the Valley frequently still enjoy the same kind of Pwlldu magic that children down the years have enjoyed. True, modern life makes it prudent for them to stay together, and some boundaries have to be set and some rules enforced. But they can still make dens; the wonderful safe beach is there for them to swim, surf, sail and ski in; the deep, clear rock pools are teeming with a myriad forms of sea life waiting to be examined and identified; crabs, lobsters and giant prawns are there to be caught; midnight swims, barbecues . . . the list is endless. As my youngest grand-child once said – *"Pwlldu is the bestest place in all the world!"*

Our forbears have maintained this glorious area for centuries, we cannot 'call back yesterday, bid time return', and few would wish to do so: change was due. It is so easy to romanticise the old life, but like life in all centuries there was good and bad. What we can do is learn from the steadfastness of the past and make sure that this small, intimate Valley, which is so very vulnerable, is not encroached upon. Pwlldu which has thrilled and delighted so many previous generations, must remain as it is, so that many more people in future years, can continue to live, visit, and appreciate 'this Eternal Place'.

Author's Note on Sources

The chief primary sources for this book are the personal recollections and memorabilia in the possession of the many people I have talked to, together with various documents, manuscripts and maps listed below:

MAPS:

1844 Tithe Map of Bishopston and Apportionment Schedules. West Glamorgan Archive Service: P/103/4/1, 2.

Duke of Beaufort's Estate Map, 1802. WGAS: D/D Beau E/1.

MANUSCRIPTS AND DOCUMENTS:

Census of England and Wales – enumerator's returns for Pennard and Bishopston: 1841, 1851, 1861, 1871, 1881, 1891.

The Pennard Parish Register.

The Bishopston Parish Register.

Pennard Church Minute Book, 1869-1957.

Surveys of Manor of Pennard and Fees of Lunnon, Kittle and Trywthfa, Gower. 1583, 1650, and 1687. WGAS: D/D MG12.

Survey of Gower and Kilvey 1764 – Gabriel Powell, WGAS: D/D MG 13.

The Timothy Collection, University College of Swansea Archives.

Gower Survey (c.1821), WGAS: D/D MG14.

Letter asking pardon for catching crabs and lobsters, 1752, WGAS: D/D MG 10.

The V. C. Boyle Collection, Bideford Maritime Museum.

The Kennelly Collection, North Devon Athenaeum.

Mariner's Mirror (Quarterly Journal Soc. for Nautical Research), Vol. 50. No. 1, Feb., 1964.

NEWSPAPERS:

The Cambrian (1804-1930).

The North Devon Journal.

Bideford Gazette.

By way of Acknowledgment I list below some of the secondary sources which I have found helpful:

Gower Society Journals: Vol. 25 (H. R. J. Davies on Pennard 1800-1973); Vol. 26 (W. N. Jenkins on Last Hours of the 'Caesar'); Vol. 25 (W. N. Jenkins on Limestone Quarrying at Pwlldu); Vol. 36 (L. A. Toft on The Gower Lime Burning Industry).

Ships and Harbours of Exmoor – Grahame Farr.

Devon Shipping, Trade and Ports (1600-1689) – Alison Grant.

An Illustrated History of Lynton and Lynmouth – John Travis.

Lime Burning – Daphne Challocombe and Geoffrey Walters.

The Maritime History of Devon, Vol. 11, Paper 4.

North Devon Shipping, Trade and Ports (1786-1939) – Basil Greenhill and Michael Nix.

Agriculture of Devon 1808 – Vancouver.

Smuggling in the Bristol Channel, 1750-1850 – Graham Smith (1989).

History of Bishopston – G. R. Orrin.

The Parish and Church of St Mary, Pennard, Gower – H. R. J. Davies and L. A. Toft.

On the Waterfront – Gareth A. Mills.

The Story of Pwlldu

by

A. I. JENKINS

pronunsed[1] by the Gower people Pwll.die about 400 years ago. the high Water mark just above the bridge, river runing out in the centre of the bay all sand where the Houses and beach is now limestone rocks on the west side of the bay making it about half size of what it is now. Mumbles a small village. a band of Brittany fisherman settled in and around pwlldie they found that Gower was a rocky place. but they was a clever lot of people, they made houses out of old Ship-wrecks the roofs they made of Sedge their inside decoration was lime. and sanded floors, they built 6 Lime Killns in the rounds and burnt lime for the land. and worked the land with donkey and ponys.

(they kept Goates for milk and cheese. and bees for honey.) The corn was cut with hocks, and thyse[2]. and later syke and cradle, then thresed the corn with the broken stick by the light of Tallow candles, then erected a mill by the stream 1/4 mile above the bridge and ground the corn taking it with donkeys pony and the small carts,across the stream up through the woods to Merchants cross.

They Brewed Beer for their people, the runners of the blackberry Bushes was cut trimed and dried for basket making. shipping the limestone to Devonshire, Barnstapl being the main centre. the vessles come out over Barnstapl bar. at half tide, and tack and drift down channel with the tide towards Lundy and after the dead tide at Low water, tack and drift up channel with the tide, met with the 4 ore[3] boats pulling and manovered in position for loading.

1 pronunsed – pronounced.
2 hocks and thyse – hooks and scythes.
3 ore – probably oar, i.e. rowing boats.

Mr. A. I. Jenkins.
(Photograph by courtesy of G. Morgan).

when Loaded the Vessles go back same way, the waste from the quarys being put on the sand which is the beach today, thus claiming pwlldu from the sea, and forcing the river where it is now. building the Ship Inn. Brew House. Beaufort Arms. Star Inn.Huntsman Inn. Church. Chapple and Monistry. the Village at High Pennard where they sunk their well for water. the big Villages at Widegate. the cottage in Heal Lane. the House at Bacon Hole. the cottage in the Valley. Chitterpies Nest. the House on the cliffs over looking the Valley. the House just before Smugglers Lane. the smugglers getting busy now the underground passage from one of the caves to one of the farms. so cleverly and Skillfully planed. so well concealed and guarded that it must many sleepless nights for Coastguards and police. it was so clevery done that it should remain so. The Skifs dredding for oysters was increasing in numbers. at the hight of the dredging there was well over 200 Skifs employing 4 each. sending their oysters to the big towns by rail.

early morning at Southend Mumbles getting the crews ready for dredging. waiting for their mates you hear the to the tune of Wait for the Waggon

> hear come the dredgers
> from High pennard and pwlldu
> pwlldu men are in the Search
> High pennard men close by

the oyster dredgers and the Quary men are the same lot. so many months dredging and so many months quarrin. a compition with the captains of the vessels for how[4] should get the Bounty cargo, the 21 st cargo. that is some idea of the quantity of Limestone shipped from Pwll die year after year.

the Greek Barque that was wrecked in Bantam, west of pwlldu. the crew sleeping on floors of the Houses their first job each morning was sharpening their Knifs. so the people of pwlldu was Happy when they left. the wreck ment work for the natives Salving[5], Copper Bolts. the first 4 mast iron Ship, the Lemansagan[6], that went to wreck on Bickin head with 2 yrs supply of provision abord. The skifs had good catches at that time not all being oysters, a forge was erected under Bickin head for sharpening tools. and the ship broken up. that ment a lot of work for the people again,

now the Cezar, a ship with 320 pressmen battend down in the holds, was run ashore at Graves End, the bodies was buried at graves end, 120 in one grave, between the spool[7] and Bickin Head. some years later a hut was erected and men digging by the graves. an old man so it from the top of Bickin and went down to see what they were doing. Hallo. what a. B.

---

4 how – who.

5 Salving – salvaging.

6 Lemansagan – Lammershagen (see 'Wrecks and Wrecking', page 173).

7 spool – I have been unable to trace this location but it is obviously the small hill to the east of Graves End.

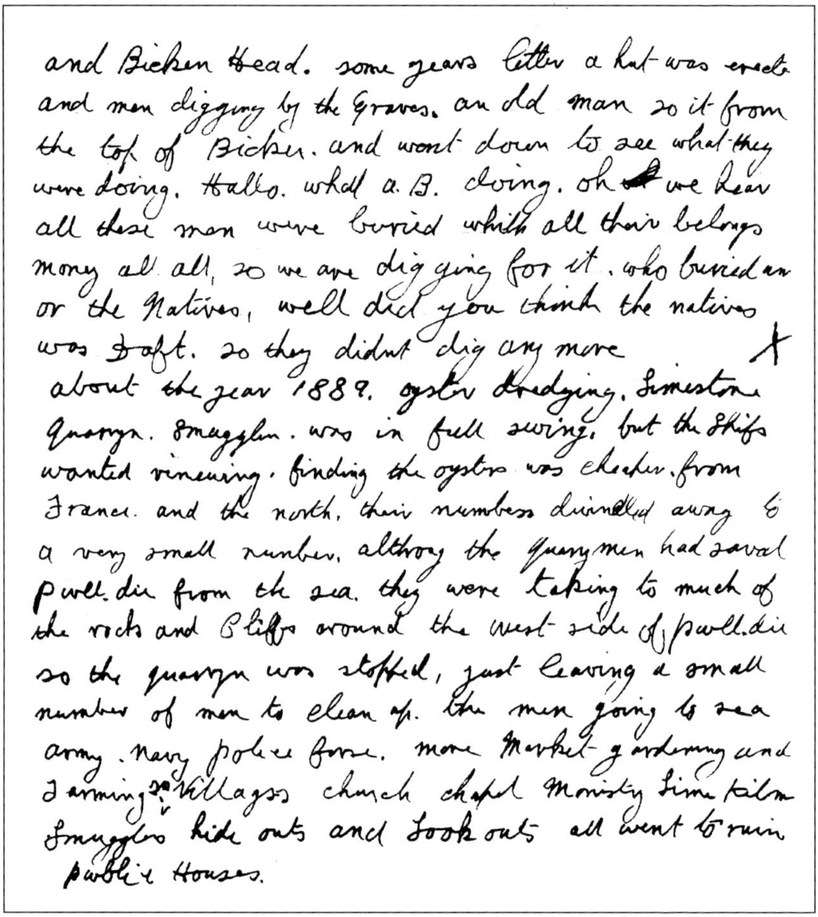
and Bicken Head. some years latter a hut was erecte
and men digging by the Graves. an old man so it from
the top of Bicker. and wont down to see what they
were doing. Hallo. what a. B. doing. oh we hear
all these men were buried whith all their belongs
mony all all, so we are dig ging for it. who buried um
or the Natives, well did you think the natives
was Daft. so they didnt dig any more X
about the year 1889. oyster dredging. Limestone
Quarryn. Smugglin. was in full swing, but the Skifs
wanted reneuing. finding the oysters was cheaper. from
France. and the north, their numbers dwindled away to
a very small number. althoug the Quarrymen had saved
pwll.du from the sea. they were taking to much of
the rocks and Cliffs around the west side of pwll.du
so the quarryn was stopped, just leaving a small
number of men to clean up. the men going to sea
army. navy police force. more Market gardening and
Farming. so Villages church chapel Ministry Lime kilns
Smugglers hide outs and Look outs all went to ruin
public Houses.

A sample page from Mr. Alf Jenkins's notebook.

doing. oh we hear all these men were buried with all their belongs money and all, so we are digging for it. who buried um. oh the natives.
well did you think the natives was daft. so they didnt dig any more.
about the year 1889 oyster dredging, Limestone quarryn, smugglin was in full swing.
but the skifs wanted renewing. finding the oysters was cheaper from France and the north, their numbers dwindled

away to a very small number, althoug the quarymen had saved pwll du from the sea, they were taking to much of the rocks and Cliffs around the west side of pwll die so the quarryn was stopped, just leaving a small number of men to clean up, the men going to sea,army,navy, police force, more market gardening and farming, so villages church chapel Monisty, Lime kilms, smugglers hide outs and lookouts, public Houses all went to ruin. more work for the quarrymen Salving the cargo of pit props. and taking them up the Hill on timber carraiges to Clyne Collery

my first recoliction of pwll die was the Old Lady Rachel[8] Timothy living in the old House at the bottom of the Hill, later picking Broad Beans in her garden in front of the House. the small Sailing ship the Tom wrecked at Bulls Bay east side of pwll die. The men making holes inthe Limeston Rock with the Jumber[9] a 6ft iron with a chisle end. blacisting it of with powder and breaking it up with 28lb Sledges and putting it out on Sleigh cars. and poneys through the East Middle and West car Roads, which was cut in the rocks, and piling it in heaps on the sand at Half tide ready for loading, it was a pretty sight with the women with their Red turnovers and Bonnets and the men in Bar fracts and Close leather caps and manovering the Vessels in position, 15 men and Women Hevers starts to load when they could start on the heep of stone just over their knes in water, when the tide is going out, in just over 6 Hours. and the Vessel is Loaded with 100 tons of Limeston, big mony for that 2/6 per Head. A painting by ~~alf Parkman~~ p.Schenk 1889 of the last 2 Vessels trading to pwlldie the last Vessel was the Maregret Davies of Barnstaple that finished about 1898. pretty to to see the frst 2 small batches of Skiffs going down by to their fishing grounds. but a sadder story now to see the Skiffs getting less in Number until they dissapered alltogether, Pwll die the boats broken up for fire the winchs a lot of the sleigh cars, especialy the ons with the 2ft weel, Saw Pit fillled in BoatHouse taken down,

8 Old Lady Rachel – this would be John and Rachel's daughter who lived on at the cottage after the death of her parents.

9 Jumber – jumper (see page 37).

all that remains now of the once busy bay iron in the rock the used to hold the Ships boats and Winches. Now the men fishing with the netts. fun for us young ones. picking up the fish as they come to the shore before the netts. The men having to wait until the tide went out, as the netts was to full of fish to pull ashore.deck cargo of coconets that was washed in all the crevices, ment a lot of work for us boys cutting out the cirnless[10] we called it Coconut Cove. the showl of spratts that came in in and aroun Pwlldie, all the pools and crevises was full of them, tons and tons a prety sight espicarly in the night light taler[11] the small ketch the Jane went to wreck west side of Bicken the deck cargos of the Norway pitprops thousands of them, it ment a lot of work salvigin them,then letten the Deck cargo fo French pit props. Now before we leave the Bay, a prediction by the older quarry men, in as many years as it took to claim pwlldu from the sea, the Sea would claim it back. Thers is 80 yds of the Beach gone in my time
The fallin trees in the Valley was cut in to logs and pulled up to pennard church, then on Timber carriags to Bishopston and made into carts gambos and gates for the farmers. This making a good parth in the Valley where you could ride a Bycycle in some places, but now in a very bad state of neglet, paths broken away trees fallen across the parths and bushes grown over the paths it is a shame that the Beautyful Vally should be left so, the Farmers Rabbit Shoot 25 guns and wel over 30 Beaters, killing over 200 Rabbits in their days Shoot. Met at Lockway in the Valley with their lunch,their Dinner at pwlldie after their sing song Stop. Tofs with their poneys and Traps Carraige and pairs with their Candle lamps goin up the Hill to Bishopston. Mumbles and Swansea, a pretty sight.
M Lloyd taking loads of fern just behind Rachel's old House up over the Cliff to Knapp Farm, Billy Ball bring the 4 in Hand to pwlldu, the Storm that washed the old plank Bridge up into the Valley(1887) replaced by a plank bridge this time with a Hand rain[12] (a Painting by Schenk). Farmers making

10 cirnless – kernels.
11 taler – later (just a slip in writing).
12 hand rain – hand rail (see painting, page 33).

Hay in the Meadows aboave the Bridge the collors of Ins[13] by the River above the Bridge, a very pretty sight, but now Meadow full of Weeds Bushes and trees, River full of weeds Bushes and trees, banks of Mud, Irises gon flood gate gone Break water in the river gone, what a diffrent picture. The Great Storm that hid pwll.die about 1911, chickens pigs brought into the kitchens to save them from the flood, sweeping the water out of the Houses with the brooms, it washed the Coadstguards path in and around pwlldu in some places 15 - 20yds it really altered the coast line

(Now the phesant shoot pretty to see the birds with their lovely colours)
The Sheep washing the Farmers bringing their flocks with their well trained dogs. and washing the Sheep in the pool in the Stream tending the Market Leaving the Market 11.30[14] at night and finding the flood down, leaving the trap by the River, and taking the poney around the Cliff path, then across the Beach, not so bad, sometimes the tide ussulling[15] having to swim the pony across the River, not so good, as it took a long time to dry fur Catching prawns Crabs and Lobsters, picking winkles Laverbread collecting Sea weed for the gardins. Supplying the Swansea and port Tabot dry docks with Set Rods, but it is all changed now Now the preparations for the Xmas and New Year partys, the large brick ovens (where they baked the Bread) full of Xmas cake the Huge soppers[16] that was used for brewing beer, full of Xmas puddings for the Nebours and Friends dancing the Hornpipes, Reels and Country dances to the Music of the Accordion and Fiddle some expert Step dancers to, now comer the Motor Bus Lorry and Motor Vals[17] Coal, oil, Minerels provisions Confectioners baker Beer. All goods delivered to the doors, now everything the pwll.die folks need has to be carried here, Making ice cream, catering for the Visitors, the farmers Ham & egg

13 collors of Ins – colours of irises.
14 Leaving the Market 11.30pm – probably after a few drinks at the pub!
15 ussulling – probably when the tide is fully in they could not cross the beach.
16 soppers – coppers.
17 Vals – could be vans.

teas,SaladTeas Frut & iccream teas etc. now a thing of the past, I never thought it was possible to see pwll die in such a terrible State of Neglet, dangerious abrouches[18] to the Bridge, Roads dangerious even to walk on paths all grown over, wherever you look theres Weeds bushes and trees, harbouring Rats Snakes and Toies, and unfourtunale Me Heath[19] wound allow me to do much about it, there is no doubt that my Story will bring Many pleasant Memories of all my Frinds who spent so many Happy times, at pwlldu some now I am Sorry to say is unable to make the jurny it will also give the younger folk some idea of the Costums and joly time at pwlldie we have appealed to the Council to do a little the road on the Hill, so we can get a bag of coal down for the Winter, but so far the only reply is the usual your Rates are payable on Dimand if and of the councils or any one concered will come from Pyle Corner through the Lane, then walk down the Hill to the Bridge they like the Britteny Fisher men, will see for themselves that Gower is a Rocky place.

The Mumble Riggta. the big yats The Shamroch and White Heather rounding the Mark at pwlldu

They grow hop Vines and Grape Vines garden a picture

Land Marks gone Ash.Tree and top pillars

The women going to Market with their poneys and pack saddles, coming home from Swansea with the buss and being brought to the top of Pwlldie Hill.

The Sleigh cars was used by the Farmers. J phillips. J Webb.W Richards W Evans R Hughes bring their prouduce for Market down High Pennard Hill and changing to their traps going up pwlldu hill to Swansea.The Sleigh Cars was used by the Farmers of High Pennard to bring their produce for Market to the Cart House that was erected by the Bridge where they changed to their traps and took their goods up pwlldu Hill, to Swansea

The Bidding weddings the women with their Bonnetts and paisley shawls and long dresses reaching to the ground men in high hats and long tail coats dancing the old Step dances, and moving a drop of Beer, lively times

18 abrouches – approaches.

19 Me Heath – my health (towards the end of his life Alf became very frail with severe arthritis in his hands.

Some interesting facts that have come to hand since publication

page 104:

One of the interesting visitors that made their way to my door was the nephew of the little lad, Wilfred Davies who had drowned so tragically in the 'black pool' which forms when a high tide has driven the stones into a solid wall and the water from the stream cannot escape into the sea. Apparently his uncle's death had never been referred to in the family and even as a small boy he was aware of some tragedy but had never been able to get any details. Quite by chance my book was sent to him as a present and he was amazed to read of his uncle's drowning. On my advice he went to the Reference Library and found that the Coroner's Report had been printed in full in the *South Wales Daily Post* of 6th August, 1908. The final remark of the Coroner is interesting: "The opinion prevails in the district that the pool should be filled in. The water in it is practically stagnant and the steep slopes of shingle that formed the sides of the bank constitute a real danger to children."

This part of the beach has always attracted children, many of whom try to shift the stones for the river to break through. When it does escape the gush of water that grows faster by the minute is a most exciting sight and draws children like a magnet but there is little doubt that it is a very dangerous place. However, I would hate to see 'the Gut' filled in as it is part of the magic of Pwlldu.

Pages 152 & 153:

Mrs. Ada Bagge (née James) was Frank James's sister and not Arthur Whopham's eldest daughter. Ada's two sisters, Ruth and Maud, took over the running of Beaufort. Lydia was not their sister but a relation of Arthur Whopham. I am grateful to Margaret Hold, sister of Molly and Dorothy James, for sending me this information. Mrs. Ada Bagge's son, Terry, was shot down in Palestine some time in the early thirties, not during the Second World War.

Page 158 (Acknowledgement of Trespassers on Rocks and Lands at Bishopston and Pennard – transcription to aid understanding):

Whereas we whose names are hereunto subscribed have severally Catched Crabs and Lobsters in the Rocks and on the Salt Sounds within the Manors of Pennard and Bishopston which do belong to his grace the Duke of Beaufort as Lord of the Said Manors, and committed other Trespasses there for which we Severally declare our Sorrow and humbly beg his grace's pardon and forgiveness And do Severally promise to pay to his grace the sum of Sixpence at the feast of St. Michael the Archangel yearly as an Acknowledgement of his Grace's right to the said Rocks and Sands for so long as we are permitted to Catch such Crabs and Lobsters or have any other Liberty thereupon As Witness our hands this 27th. day of May 1732.

David Hughes — John Taylor — Daniel Taylor
John Jenkin — (the mark of) Robert Jones
John David — Jenkin Donne — Benjamin Beynon
(the mark of) William Hawkin
(the mark of) John David

Page 179:
Photograph of *S.S. Tours* kindly sent to me by Miss Margaret Webborn, a direct descendant of John Timothy the diarist, whose two grand-daughters are in the picture (Kathleen, 3rd from the left, Rose, 5th from the right). They had walked from Mumbles to Hunt's Bay in order to witness the great event.

Page 191:
THE NIGHT THE GERMANS INVADED PWLLDU!
When Ernie Tucker was asked what he would do "if the Germans really did come in here" – he had little idea that Germans did come into the bay and on many different occasions!

A young girl who lives locally was spending a year in Germany. In the flat below lived a German couple who had been extremely kind to her. On the occasion of her Mother visiting her daughter, the older German couple invited mother and daughter to their flat for drinks. Although the German's command of English was limited he could easily follow the conversation.

He was interested as to where the Welsh guests lived. He was told that they lived near the coast of Gower – the nearest bay being Pwlldu. His guests were surprised at his reaction when he heard this name. "Yes, I know," came the reply. He hurriedly left the room and quickly returned carrying a large sheet of yellowing paper which was revealed as a shipping chart. Pointing excitedly at the South Wales coastline his finger came to rest on the bay of Pwlldu. "Water, water – always good water!" he exclaimed.

In spite of his limited use of English, a remarkable story unfolded. He had been a 'U' boat captain during the Second World War. Apparently it was not unusual for German 'U' boats to land in secret, usually at night, on various parts of the West Wales coast in order to take on fresh water supplies. Pwlldu was considered perfect for this manoeuvre on a number of counts – it was a deep bay, protected by high cliffs and had a perfect fresh water supply from the stream which wound its way right down to the beach. By means of a series of words and gestures the Captain explained how a long line was extended from the boat into the river and fresh water taken on board. The 'U' boat would then slide out of the bay under the cover of darkness. As their German host said with a twinkle of laughter in his eyes, "Coastguards – always sleeping!"

Acknowledgements

This book is largely the outcome of numerous conversations with men and women whose families had lived and worked in Pwlldu and its environs for many years. They not only shared their memories but in many cases supplied me with small black and white snaps from their precious family albums, which I have used to illustrate their stories. Some of these people have been named in the text; the reader like the writer is indebted to them all: Mr Billy Ace, Mr Eddie Butcher, Mrs Phyllis Blewett, Mrs Sandra Davies, Mrs Sheila Edwards, Mr Walter Griffiths, Mrs Queenie Heath, Mr Gwynfor Hughes, Mrs Sarah Thomas James, Mr Alf Jenkins, Mrs Mary Ann Jenkins, Miss Lily Jenkins, Mr Hezekiah Jenkins, Mr Allan Jones, Mr Arthur Jones, Mr Ivor Jones, Mr David Jones, Mrs Dorothy Jones, Mr Graham Jones, Mr Paul Jones, Mr Gareth Mills, Mr Arthur Owen, Mrs Ivy Owen, Mr Arthur Phillips, Mr Harry Phillips, Mrs Connie Richards, Mrs Vivienne Rudall, Mr Brian Simpson, Mrs Merle Simons, Miss Rosslyn Stephens, Mrs Margaret Snell, Mr Peter Thomas, Mr George Whitehead, Mrs Dorothy Williams, Mrs Mollie Winter.

Thanks are due to Dr W. N. Jenkins for permission to reproduce photographs from his collection

I am indebted to Mr Colin Phipps for his help in restoring old photographs used in the 'sheep washing' section.

I am deeply grateful to the librarians, archivists and curators of many institutions including: Miss Susan Beckley and her staff at the West Glamorgan Achives; Mrs Elisabeth Bennett, archivist, University of Wales, Swansea; Mrs Liza Osborne, Swansea Reference Library; Mrs Marilyn Jones, The Cambrian Indexing Project; Mrs Joy Slocombe, Ilfracombe Museum, Mrs Pat Wiggett, North Devon Museum Trust, the staff of the Athenaeum, Barnstaple.

I owe a particular debt to Mrs Barbara McGaughey and members of my family, for reading my manuscript and making constructive suggestions for its improvement.

I am grateful to Mr Raymond Heath of Icon Computer Services for advice and help.

A special thank-you to my grand-daughter, Miss Jenni Heath for her line sketches illustrating the smuggling section.

I thank Mr Donald Martin and the staff at Dinefwr Press for helping me every step of the way towards the final production of this attractive book.

Most of all, I am grateful to Lawrence, my husband, for his support and practical help. I would not have been able to write this book without him.

The Name 'Pwlldu'

Readers will note that the spelling of Pwlldu changes throughout the narrative. I have used the version of the name which appears on the various historical documents under discussion.

It is unusual to find a Welsh name surviving in this very English part of Gower. There are two possible explanations of its derivation. The English translation of the Welsh 'Pwlldu' is 'Black Pool'. Some think it refers to the actual shape of the bay, which is rounded and deep; certainly when the sun leaves the bay, which it does quite early, looking from the top of the steep sided cliffs on either side, the cove does indeed resemble a huge black pool. Another explanation, subscribed to by many of the older local inhabitants, is that the name refers to the pool which is formed under the Eastern cliff when the stream has been impounded by the ridge of rounded pebbles. Similar names with similar derivations exist in Cornwall – 'Poldhu', and in Brittany – 'Le Pouldu', and of course, the well-known English 'Blackpool'.